the complete

Dachshund

the complete

Dachshund

bruce hutchinson

and dee hutchinson

HOWELL
BOOK
HOUSE

MACMILLAN is a registered trademark of Macmillan, Inc.

Howell Book House
A Simon & Schuster Macmillan Company
1633 Broadway
New York, NY 10019

Library of Congress Cataloging-in-Publication Data
Hutchinson, Bruce, 1937–
     The Complete Daschund / Bruce Hutchinson and Dee Hutchinson.
       p.   cm.
ISBN 0-87605-135-2
1. Daschunds.   I. Hutchinson, Dee.   II Title.
SF429.D25H86   1997
636.753'8—dc21

Manufactured in the United States of America

10 9 8 7 6 5 4 3 2 1

For my mother Nancy F. Onthank and my father Pierce who put up with us both, Jeannette W. Cross, Romona and Kippy Van Court, and John Hutchinson Cook without whose knowledge, guidance, and love this book would not have been possible, and of course the many Dachshunds we have owned and bred, which have brightened our lives, and hopefully those of others.

Contents

Foreword

Writing a book on Dachshunds reminds us of the thought we used to put into our children's Christmas stockings. Too small, and they would be disappointed. Too large, and we faced the dilemma of how to fill them.

Since too small was unacceptable, we had to balance its content with a mixture of goodies, necessities, and fillers. We are not dealing with alpha and omega here, or a clever tale filled with numerous plot twists. We are relating both objective and subjective impressions of long, little dogs with short legs and large hearts which will wend their way into yours. We hope that our attempt to share the gift of our love and knowledge of this animal with you will be as accepted as the Christmas stockings were by our children. The fun and exciting, the utilitarian, and the mundane, are the ingredients essential to understanding and appreciating the Dachshund.

While we approach this book with enormous enthusiasm and excitement, we are humbled by the reality that for every Dachshund owner there are a like number of opinions and experiences surrounding the breed. We offer only our love and knowledge of the dog from our perspective to those considering owning one. We do not seek to offend or challenge those equally as knowledgeable.

Accordingly, we make no claims to being the sole authority on this lovable little dog. Throughout, we have sought to glean knowledge and anecdotes from others in the hope of being specific enough to entice, excite, and educate the first time owner or breeder, and generic enough to be of interest and enjoyment to all.

This is not a rehash of material on Dachshunds written by others; hence, a limited bibliography. The photographs contained herein are a selection of Dachshunds that we consider excellent specimens of the breed. In order to avoid offending anyone, we have used pen-and-ink drawings where appropriate to interpret the strong and weak points of the Dachshund's conformation from our perspective.

Acknowledgments

We owe our thanks to the many true Dachshund people who have contributed their knowledge, artwork, and photographs to this book. While impossible to acknowledge all by name we offer the following who, through major time, effort and love of the breed, have contributed significantly to this text.

David Blum is an Affiliate Professor at the University of Washington. He is a symphony conductor, and a lover and owner of Dachshunds for over five decades.

Carrie Hamilton was raised with Dachshunds as pets. In 1979, her parents purchased their first "show" dogs, a male and female from the same litter. She became interested in Field and Den Trialing and participated in these activities for several years with her Dachshunds. She was approved to judge Field Trials in 1990 and Den Trials (Earthdog Trials) in 1992.

Mary Sue Humphries has been showing Dachshunds since 1970. Her first show dog was a Miniature smooth. A chance encounter with a silver dapple Miniature smooth in 1971 led to a lifelong love for the "colored" Miniature longhair. Since 1974 she has been breeding Miniature longhairs under the Barbomac kennel name. Mary Sue is the founder and a charter member of the Central Ohio Dachshund Club; a life member of the Dachshund Club of America; and a member of the National Miniature Dachshund Club, the Pharaoh Hound Club of America, and the American Dog Owner's Association.

John Jeanneney bred his first litter of von Moosbach wirehaired Dachshunds in 1968. Seven years later he received a special research license from the New York State Department of Environmental Conservation to begin an experimental program of using leashed tracking dogs to find wounded deer. The Deer Search organization grew out of this research project, in good part due to the timely successes of his wirehaired Dachshund Fld. Ch. Clary von Moosbach who was an outstanding Field Trial dog.

By the end of 1955 John had found 136 wounded deer with tracking dogs. This gave him an opportunity to form ideas about what is required of a Dachshund that works above ground under difficult conditions of weather and terrain. At present, John lives with his wife Jolanta, who is also a Dachshund breeder, in Clinton Corners, New York. Together they continue breeding Dachshunds mentally and physically suited for arduous work in the field.

David Kawami became intrigued by wirehaired Dachshunds while stationed at the U.S. Army 130th Station Hospital in Heidelberg, Germany. It would be a number of years before he and his wife Trudy would have their first wire. By a quirk of fate this first wire was a French import from a kennel that concentrated on Field and underground work. It took a year of watching this wirehaired Dachshund, Versailles des Trois Hures, also called Willow, to understand this was not like any dog he had ever known. Fortunately, Field and Den Trials were discovered, and the little dog finally made sense. The dog household is now five, four Field Champions and a Dual Champion. Two hold Obedience Titles, and all but the youngest have titles in go-to-ground work. In the late spring and summer, the Dachshunds assist farmers in underground pest control. The Dual Champion is also used to track wounded deer for New York State's Deer Search program. Mr. Kawami is a Dachshund Field Trial judge, member of the Dachshund Club of America, and was Chairman of the Trial Advisory Council from 1992–1994. He is also a member of the Dachshund Association of Long Island, and the Kings County Kennel Club.

Jane Larsen has been training dogs since high school. Prior to becoming involved with Dachshunds, she and her husband George raised, trained and showed Basenjis for a number of years under the kennel name "Cock's Crow." Jane first came under the spell of a Dachshund when she met the fiery little Standard longhair, O.T.Ch. Mayrhofen Olympischer Star L—the first member of the Hound Group to become an Obedience Trial Champion. With the purchase of a puppy out of this remarkable bitch in 1977, the family joined the ranks of those who are blissfully "owned by a Dachshund." Their first litter was sirened by Ch. & O.T.Ch. Himark Vanquish, TD—the first Dachshund to hold championships in both conformation and Obedience. Descendants of this union comprise the IVIC family of Dachshunds in the Larsen household today. Jane strongly believes in the importance of maintaining sound mental, as well as physical, qualities in the breed and enjoys participating in a variety of performance activities with her own dogs.

Professor Iris Cornelia Love is a noted historian, writer, lecturer and photographer. She was brought up by a Scottie, a Boxer, five Skye Terriers, a Poodle, a Great Dane and a mixture. She has owned smooth Dachshunds since 1961. Of the six bitches she has acquired since 1986, five were shown, and all became champions. Since 1990, she has bred three litters from two different bitches. Fourteen puppies were born, of these nine were shown, and all obtained their championships. Her smooth bitch, Ch. Dachsmith Love's

Tyche Tyche, won Best of Breed at Westminster in 1996, and was the number one smooth Dachshund bitch in 1992, 1993, 1994 and 1995. Professor Love's dogs have made canine history as two from the same litter, Ch. Dachsmith Love's Tyche Tyche and Ch. Dachsmith Love's Ajax, have won Best in Show in all breed competition, Tyche Tyche in 1994 and Ajax in 1996.

Dr. Kit Walker, veterinarian and life-long Dachshund fancier, is currently a small animal practitioner and practice owner in Omaha, Nebraska. She and her Dachshunds have been active participants in her assisted therapy for ten years, making regular visits to area nursing homes and hospitals. She is also a strong advocate of Obedience training, and has been very fortunate to have two dachsies train her, very patiently, to five titles, the highest to date being a CDX. No one questions her devotion to the breed, as evidenced by the Dachshund paraphernalia dotting her home. She is grateful for being asked to contribute to this book, especially because it "immortalizes" her beloved mini, Harriet.

The authors relaxing at Lake Tahoe.

About the Authors

Shortly before Dee and Bruce Hutchinson were married in 1958, she made a promise to him that she would never breed or show Dachshunds. Bruce understandably had his doubts; after all, Dee was the daughter of Nancy Onthank, a famous and respected breeder and judge of Dachshunds, and the founder of Rose Farm Kennels. As a young child, Dee was heavily involved with the dogs—participating in the breeding, whelping, showing, grooming, and general care of her mother's Dachshunds.

Dee was introduced to Dog Shows through Junior Handling where she trained her mother's puppies. At the age of sixteen, she finished third in the Junior Handling competition at the Westminster Dog Show held at Madison Square Garden in New York. When she was eighteen, she handled her mother's smooth Dachshund, Ch. Venture of Hardway, to Best in Show at the Greenwich Kennel Club.

Having only briefly seen his newborn daughter in the hospital before returning to Fort Eustis, Virginia as a lieutenant in the U.S. Army, Bruce was excitedly awaiting the arrival of Dee and the baby to join him in their new home. The expression of anticipation on his face quickly turned to one of horror when Dee emerged from the car with a baby in one arm and a male Dachshund in the other. It didn't help when Jeannette W. Cross, one of the true matriarchs of the Dachshund world, appeared from the passenger side.

"Why?" he said, "You promised."

"Danny is an older dog," she replied, "and needs a good home."

After a brief exchange of deleted expletives, Bruce forgot the dog and gave all of his attention to his new daughter. After all, every young family needs a dog and this one was too old to be shown.

Six months later Dee returned to Fort Eustis after a trip to Greenwich to see her mother. She gleefully jumped from the car with baby and Gigi, a female Dachshund. For Danny, it was love at first sight. Some time later they

"This is absolutely my first work. I am not in the field of art. This is a product from my heart because I need him to be my remembrance and would like to let the world know how much I love him." Thana Achariyawan, Bangkhen, Thailand

had five puppies. The foundation was born. Life would never be the same again.

For the next few years, Dee became extensively involved with her dogs, traveling to dog shows every weekend, while Bruce stayed home to baby-sit for their children and take care of Dee's small, but growing, kennel. It became a true test of their marriage, with a "love 'em or leave 'em" choice. Bruce's defenses crumbled, and his long relationship with Dachshunds began. He has subsequently bred and whelped Dachshunds, and even judged a Dachshund Match Show.

Over the next thirty-five years, to help maintain his independence and sanity, Bruce found the time to become an avid skier and sailor. He is a self-taught celestial navigator, and has navigated sailboats over more than 10,000 miles of ocean including trips through the Panama Canal and to the Arctic. Through the years he has written several published articles on navigation, and many articles on dogs.

While Bruce was skiing in Vermont, Colorado and Utah, or surviving storms in the North Atlantic Ocean, Dee was building her reputation as a respected breeder and handler of dogs, having bred well over 100 Champion Dachshunds of all varieties and both sizes during her career. After many years of handling several different breeds, and living and working with professional handlers in the "trenches" of the dog show world, she decided to try her hand at judging beginning with Dachshunds, and continuing on to all the Hound Breeds. Today she is licensed to judge five groups and Best in Show.

Judging assignments have enabled Dee and Bruce to travel extensively to dog shows throughout South America, Bermuda, Canada, Denmark, Japan, New Zealand, and Australia, as well as the entire United States. In 1995, Dee was honored to be able to judge the hound group at the Westminster Kennel Club.

While they both continue to enjoy sailing, skiing, and five grandchildren, their involvement with dogs in general, and Dachshunds in particular, has not waned. Dee continues to breed, show, and judge. As a long-standing member of the Board of Directors of the Dachshund Club of America, she continues to devote her time and counsel to all who would seek knowledge of the Dachshund.

"Vivian," the authors' Miniature longhair Dachshund bunkmate enjoying a day of sailing on the Long Island Sound.

chapter 1

The Long and Short of It

It will soon become evident to you that we adore Dachshunds. Over the nearly forty years that we have been breeding, showing, judging, loving, and tearfully burying numbers of this remarkable breed we have acquired a good deal of knowledge about the Dachshund, and are aware that we still have much to learn.

Throughout this book, we will draw on our experiences, and that of others, to pass along practical information for living with your Dachshund. Should you require details on their conformation requirements for showing, or if you are interested in the history of the breed, we have included chapters for those purposes as well.

It's not surprising that each year, Dachshunds have consistently ranked among the top ten percent of dogs registered with the American Kennel Club. Unlike any other breed, they have an unfair advantage. There are three varieties and two sizes, resulting in six different possible combinations. The variety of color choices furthers the attractiveness of the breed.

Nothing in particular about the Dachshund makes it stand tall among other breeds, including, of course, its legs. The name comes from the German *dachs*, meaning "badger," and *hund* meaning "dog." Their size, shape, and coat made them ideal for pursuing badgers into their underground burrows. Unless you have badgers in your front lawn, your basement, or breeding under your bed, then there is really no practical reason to own a Dachshund. If you insist on owning one anyway, count on him being around for a while. While any animal is subject to premature illness, our experience has been Dachshunds live into their early teens, and one of our breeding just passed away at seventeen. Above all, be prepared to devote constant time and love to this dog. He will demand nothing less from you, and will give you much more in return.

The three varieties of Dachshunds.

The real reasons for their popularity begin with practical considerations. Depending on your requirements, there is a model to fit almost everyone's needs. Unlike other hound breeds, they don't drool, slobber, or smell (even when wet), unless of course they have been hunting in a swamp—which is entirely possible. Only the longhaired sheds, and then only as he periodically grows a new coat. Miniatures fit under your airplane seat while traveling, and Standards are easily shipped as excess baggage. Both can fit in your kitchen sink for bathing. When shaking off excess water, as all dogs will, they only get you wet from the knees down. They feel equally at home in the city or the country, an apartment or a house, indoors or outside and in hot or cold climates. Ours are sure-footed sailors who love to swim, while at least one other has skied on snow. Having such short legs, they are much closer to you when you hug them. They are excellent with children and the elderly, make good guard dogs, and require little food (though they'll try to con you out of more).

There are three varieties of Dachshunds: smooth (often incorrectly referred to as "shorthaired"), longhaired, and wirehaired. While it was generally assumed that the smooth was the original breed with longs and wires resulting from outcrossings with other breeds, historians make a strong point that all three varieties came onto the scene at the same time. It was in the 19th Century that hunters, while adapting the longhaired to their own specific needs, further refined them through selective breeding to the Cocker Spaniel, and likewise the wirehaired to the wirehaired Pinscher, Dandie Dinmont, Scottish Terrier, Skye Terrier, and wirehaired Fox Terrier. That practice has long since been discontinued, although in the United States it is permissible to crossbreed among the three varieties. The rest of the world, however only permits breeding within each variety, and recognizes each variety and size as a separate breed. As a result, outside of the United States there are six recognized Dachshund breeds.

Ch. Chopmist Lady Buxton owned by Gina Leone is shown here at age 14.

Shown at 8 years of age, "Midge," owned by Susan Jones, is just a youngster. Photo: Sidney Stafford.

Smooth Dachshund.
Drawing by Gina Leone.
Copyright 1995

Longhair Dachshund.
Drawing by Gina Leone.
Copyright 1995

If you are looking for a big dog, about all we can offer you is a very fat Dachshund. The Standard, which is the largest, weighs anywhere from sixteen to thirty pounds, with the average mature dog (male) between twenty-five and twenty-nine pounds, and the bitch (female) between eighteen and twenty-three pounds. Miniatures, as defined in the approved Dachshund Standard of the Dachshund Club of America and the American Kennel Club, weigh under eleven pounds at one year of age. This does not mean that if you buy a Miniature as a puppy he is guaranteed by the breeder to weigh under the required weight limit when he matures, it only means that he cannot be shown in the Miniature classes at a dog show. A reputable breeder will not intentionally misrepresent a Standard as being a Miniature. If you intend to purchase a Miniature for show be sure to address the weight question with the breeder prior to assuming ownership, and wait until the puppy is at least four months old.

Perhaps the most confusing (and often controversial) subject among breeders is that of color. We receive more questions from people on this than any other subject. Though common, these questions are the ones we are least able to answer in an informed manner. For that reason we have gratefully included a separate chapter on the subject (chapter 8) written by Mary Sue

Wirehair Dachshund by
Gina Leone. Copyright
1995

Humphries, an expert in the field and a highly respected breeder of Dachshunds. All color variations are discussed including brindles and dapples. While detailed and technical by necessity, it will answer your questions on an often complicated subject.

By far, the two most common and accepted colors are the red and the black and tan. It should be noted here that color is only a matter of personal choice or availability. A Dachshund's personality or temperament is not altered in any way by color.

Besides the two basic colors mentioned above, there are six additional colors currently accepted by the Dachshund Club of America and the American Kennel Club. These are: blue and tan, chocolate and tan, cream, fahn and tan, wheaten, and wild boar. While a detailed description of each color would be at best difficult and confusing, suffice it to say that there are a variety of colors available to suit your personal preference. The important point to be made is that your Dachshund must be one of the eight colors mentioned here in order for him to be accepted for registration by the AKC.

Now don't get mad and throw the book down in disgust saying, "A friend has a dapple and he is registered with the AKC!" This may very well be true, but dapple is not a color. It is a marking or pattern. Other markings or patterns are double dapple, brindle, piebald, and sable. A Dachshund may be classified by the breeder as a dapple, but if there is not a definable color, you will not be able to have him registered.

At this point, we have either totally confused you or intrigued you into learning a little more about color. Assuming both to be the case, we'll discuss this subject in more depth without sinking to the level of despair.

Of the eight possible colors, three are separate and distinct. Red is any shade or color of what most observers would consider brown with no other separate or distinguishable patches. Likewise, the cream and the wheaten (light red), have the same characteristics, except of course for their color. The wild boar, which is generally associated with the wirehaired, but also found in smooths of wire breeding, is double coated with a lighter coat underneath

Ch. Sleepytimes Exemption red Miniature longhair shown at the age of 2^1/$_2$ after winning best of variety in 1987 at the Dachshund Club of America Specialty Show. Owned by Susan Jones. *Photo: Schoolcraft.*

"My-T," a black and tan smooth, owned by Shirley Silagi.

and a black overlay. The remaining four all include the words "and tan." Tan refers to points or markings including, but not limited to, over the eyes, under the chin, on the feet, and under the tail. In other words, a pure chocolate or pure black Dachshund with no tan points, although registerable with the AKC, would be considered to have a fault in the show ring. A dapple therefore may be spotted and have different markings and colors on its body, but he must have tan points in order to qualify as to color. All of this, of course, should only be important to you if you intend to breed your dog and want to be able to register or show his offspring. We do not claim to be the ultimate authority on color, as the subject has and will continue to be debated in the future. The important point is to ask the right questions of the breeder at the time you purchase your Dachshund to insure that he can be registered under the current Dachshund Standard.

The final word on color is still evolving. Mary Sue Humphries has correctly noted that two piebald Dachshunds recently earned the title of Champion in the conformation show ring. The United States is the only country in the world where, at present, this is possible. A predominantly white dog, as often found in the piebald, is a disqualification in every other nation but here. The current Australian Dachshund Standard (as of December 1966) refers to color as follows: "Black and tan, dark brown with lighter shadings, dark red, light red, dappled, tiger-marked, or brindle. In black and tan, red, and dappled dogs, the nose and nails should be black, in chocolate they are often brown." Although not specifically mentioned, the color white is noticeably excluded.

The Kennel Club of England, however, is more specific in its definition: "All colours allowed but (except in dapples which should be evenly marked all over) no white permissible, save for a small patch on chest which is permitted but not desirable. Nose and nails black in all colours except chocolate/tan and chocolate/dapple, where brown permitted."

As second-generation breeders, we will never recognize or acknowledge piebald as an acceptable color or pattern either in the show ring or as breeding stock, regardless of any future changes to the Standard. Could it be that white was introduced to the Dachshund from the Beagle? If true, it would follow that piebald dogs can not be purebred Dachshunds. The basic coats and colors of Dachshunds have not changed in hundreds of years. Too many reputable breeders have worked for years to maintain and improve the breed. We will not condone or accept what we consider to be a type of dangerous experimentation of which the average breeder has no knowledge of

A chocolate lover's dream.
Photo: Catherine Van Ormer.

From left to right: black and tan dapple, double blue and tan dapple, and double black and tan dapple. Note reduced eye size of the double at right.

the consequences. Unrestricted "color breeding" is not acceptable in any other breed recognized by the AKC, and in our opinion, should not be acceptable in the Dachshund, when subsequent potential problems in temperament and health are unfair to the dog, their owners, and the dog world in general.

Now that you understand size, and have some knowledge of color, you will still have to decide on sex and variety before you can fit the pieces together to form your perfect dog. Sex should be easy, right? After all, you only have two choices—dog or bitch.

If you intend to breed your dog, the choice is simple—female. One should never buy a male with the intent to breed him unless, of course, you intend to enter him in dog shows and later use him for stud. Only if he is a proven Champion, or has bloodlines that a breeder needs, your dog will not be accepted for stud. We are astounded by the number of inquiries we receive from people wanting to breed their male. We try to express that what he doesn't know won't hurt him. . . once bred, a male will become macho, and to mark his territory he will begin lifting his leg to the point where every object in your house will seem like the proverbial fire hydrant. To put it plainly, he will exhibit behavior you will regret.

On the other hand, a breeder will often breed your bitch to their stud for a fee, as long as he doesn't feel that the breeding might be detrimental to "furthering the betterment of the breed." (A wonderfully broad phrase championed by the AKC and every reputable breeder.) We will make no effort here to further define or elaborate on this self-contained, succinct, unwritten law, but suffice it to say that for a fee many breeders will provide a stud service with no questions asked.

From our perspective, the only major difference between a male and a female is in the cost of having your dog neutered or your bitch spayed, which all breeders encourage unless you plan to breed. Girls are more expensive to fix than boys. (Consult your local veterinarian for prices in your area.) Aside from the inconvenience of a female in heat, and the male's periodic interest in sex, two dogs of the same sex in any breed tend to be more aggressive towards one another if they have not been fixed. Regardless of sex, however, Dachshunds will exhibit the same characteristics of love, devotion, humor, and mischief for which they have become known.

The personality of Dachshunds can differ significantly among the three varieties. The problem is trying to define different and generic traits, which—at best—can only be subjective. It is important to distinguish between personality and temperament. The two should never be considered synonymous. A separate discussion of temperament will be included in the next chapter.

Following is an attempt to generalize, based upon our experience, the different personality characteristics of the three varieties. Others who are equally knowledgeable of the breed might disagree with our observations and at the very least would be able to elaborate with anecdotes of their own. If you gain nothing more from this discussion than understanding that differences in personality do in fact exist, then we have fulfilled our charter. If you were to ask us which variety we preferred our honest answer would have to be that we hold all of them in high esteem. While different, they share common traits—intelligent and clever, rambunctious yet gentle, loving and spiteful, creative and destructive, responsive and stubborn, so smart they're experts at playing stupid. Whatever your ultimate choice, it will not be a mistake.

Perhaps it is best to liken the smooth to the control group in an experiment—it is the Standard by which everything else is measured. Figuratively speaking, it is much like the fulcrum in a see-saw. As previously mentioned,

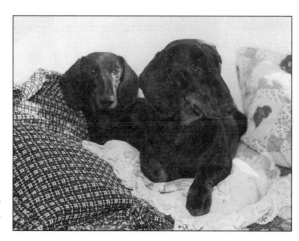

Smooth Dachshunds making themselves at home.
Photo: Leone.

the longhair was influenced by the Cocker Spaniel, and the wire by various Terriers. The smooth on the other hand seems not to have been influenced by anything other than its own evolution with its origins not totally known.

Evolving in part from the sporting breeds, the mere mention of the Cocker and Springer Spaniels, a Golden Retriever, or an Irish Setter seems to set the stage for helping to visualize the personality of the longhair variety. Adjectives such as *soft* and *good-natured* immediately come to mind. Happiest in your lap, they seem to be able to mold themselves into every available crevice on your body. As placid as they may appear, when permitted to run free, they can be voracious hunters chasing squirrels for hours at a time, and return home exhausted and hungry, wanting only to return to your lap for a well-earned nap.

A word of warning is in order about the Miniature long. For such small, gentle dogs, they can have very big mouths and well developed vocal chords, producing a high pitched "yipe" which will try anyone's patience. Although all three varieties of the Miniature tend to be more talkative than the Standard, the long seems to dominate the conversation, and the only word you can get in edgewise is a forceful "shut up," which, when effective, will put your little friend into a most temporary state of depression. The symptoms

Miniature black and tan smooth. *Photo: Ashby.*

Elegance in the snow. *Photo: Hogan.*

are predictable, short lived, and will have no lasting effect. Generally they will try to hide their head, or roll on their back and look up at you as if to say, "I'm sorry," but then when you turn away they often test you briefly once more to determine if you were serious. This minor flaw can be an asset in your home or apartment, however, as potential intruders will be quickly dissuaded from unlawful entry. They are very effective watchdogs. Ours have even awakened us at night when deer have wandered close to our home, and have saved our shrubbery and tulips from becoming a meal.

One disadvantage to owning a longhair of either size is that they do shed when growing a new coat. The amount of shedding is minor compared to other breeds, which can shed continuously. You need not be concerned that your furniture and clothing will constantly require a lint brush, particularly if you occasionally run a comb through the coat, which leads us to another consideration—grooming.

By definition, a longhair does have a long coat which will require some care on your part to keep it looking good. While constant trips to the grooming shop are unnecessary, the coat is subject to picking up unwanted foreign objects such as leaves, burrs, and other wondrous things they can find to run through or roll on. If you live in a city, or keep your dog on a leash, this will not be a major problem. But, if the dog is permitted to run loose, be warned that it does tend to act as a magnet. When a bath, drying, brushing, and combing fails, you may occasionally have to resort to a snip with the scissors. While not mandatory, this periodic care is recommended to keep this beautiful dog looking and feeling in top form. Remember to have a large towel handy for a wet longhair. They tend to absorb water.

Strongly influenced by its Terrier heritage, the wirehair tends to be feisty and macho in appearance, but is a marshmallow behind the facade. In our opinion, a correctly coated wire sheds the least out of the three varieties, as long as you follow a periodic grooming program. While different colors are available, the most common are wild boar, red, and black and tan.

At one with nature. *Photo: Hogan.*

With their coats touching ground, longhairs are a magnet for snowballs in winter.

Standard wild boar wirehair. *Photo: Susa.*

Despite its wiry coat, the wire requires considerably less grooming than the long. If your dog is intended only as a pet, you should count on a schedule of about six times a year. This depends entirely on your own preference, as many owners permit their dog's coats to become long and shaggy, grooming them as little as twice a year. We think letting a dog go too long detracts from his appearance, promotes unnecessary shedding, and is generally uncomfortable for him. Various grooming techniques are discussed later in this book.

While you may prefer the softer appearance of the long, or the traditional look of the smooth, it's hard not to love the wire. Its acceptance and popularity continues to increase as the variety becomes better known, and the demand (particularly for the Miniature) is, in some areas, exceeding the supply. Aside from their personalities, most people can't resist them as puppies.

They present as cute a picture as any breed. You may find the fuzzy ones to be the most adorable wires in the litter, but beware—these will have the smoothest, longest, and fastest growing coats as they grow older, and will subsequently require a considerable amount of grooming. The puppies with the shortest hair will generally grow to have a correct, short wire coat, and will require less grooming. At first glance, they may appear to be smooths, but upon closer examination, they will have telltale whiskers around their mouths and on their feet. Their coats will develop as they grow older, and their personalities will be the same as the fuzzy ones. In our opinion, wires are your best choice for households which include adults and children with allergies. We would particularly recommend the short, correctly coated ones discussed above, as their shedding is minimal, and their heavier coat is the least likely to become airborne.

Similar to the longhair, the Miniature wire also has a big mouth, and as such makes an excellent watchdog.

Still another great watchdog with a big mouth is the smooth—which leads us to a brief description of this mainstay of the Dachshund breed.

The smooth is probably the variety that first attracted you to Dachshunds. After all, they are the variety affectionately known as "Hot Dogs." In the world of dog shows, one of the most coveted prizes is Best of Winners. Among Dachshund fanciers it is referred to as "Best of Wieners." It is still surprising to us that many people don't realize that longs and wires are Dachshunds when they first see them, but we have never had anyone ask us what kind of dog a smooth was.

Now that we have described some of the perceived characteristics of the longs and wires, it is difficult to isolate the singular differences in the smooths. They are the ones that popularized the breed, and the longs and wires followed. Their best attribute is that their coats require little or no grooming, and shedding is not a major consideration. Their temperaments, when properly bred and raised, have been, in our experience, the most consistent, predictable, and gentle of the three varieties.

The more we have attempted to distinguish among the different characteristics of the three varieties, the more we have come to the realization that they are all Dachshunds. Beauty and personality are truly in the eye of the beholder. Now you may have a better understanding as to why we don't have a favorite, but appreciate them all.

If you don't already own a Dachshund, we hope that we have convinced you that you should. People continually return to us to either replace one they have lost after many years of love, or to add to their family of Dachshunds already at home. Most find them to be excellent companions for their larger dogs (inevitably the Dachshund becomes the boss). We don't ever remember hearing Dachshund owners say they would never own another one.

A smooth and a wire by Gina Leone.

chapter 2

Choosing a Puppy

Since the personality and temperament of any breed of dog will be influenced by a combination of heredity and environment, your Dachshund can be a spoiled brat or a well-behaved, lovable animal. In general, you can help develop his personality.

Temperament is defined by Webster as "one's natural disposition." A dog's temperament is normally the direct result of breeding. Before discussing the specifics of selecting a Dachshund, a general discussion of temperament generic to all breeds is probably the single most important factor in your choice of a dog.

So far, we have given you many options as to variety, size, and color. We have been careful not to make recommendations, as we feel the choice should ultimately be made by you. Beauty, after all, is in the lap of the beholder. Here, however, we feel obligated to voice our very strong opinion in recommending that you purchase your Dachshund from a "reputable breeder." The key word here is *reputable*. While no definition exists, as such, for a reputable breeder, they all have similar characteristics. Despite what you may pay for your puppy, they are not-for-profit individuals (show us a breeder who is in it for the money, and we will guarantee that this person is not interested in the betterment of the breed). For the most part, they are members of the Dachshund Club of America, their primary purpose in breeding is for show, their puppies are all registered with the American Kennel Club, and the pedigrees of their puppies contain several ancestors with "Ch," which is an abbreviation for Champion, preceding their names. Kennel size should not be a determining factor. There are many reputable breeders who have as little as one litter a year.

There are several reasons why you have decided to purchase a Dachshund, and the most important is probably that you like their appearance. A

15

Wire pup

Dachshund purchased from a reputable breeder will for the most part look like a Dachshund and more than likely conform to the Standard. After all, they were bred for show.

"Reputable breeder as compared to what . . ." you may ask. Simply stated, pet stores and puppy mills. We personally have nothing against pet stores. The ones we have seen are clean and the animals well cared for. They provide the needed service of supplying various grooming materials, food, dietary supplements, training materials, toys, and other items that every pet owner needs. We do not, however, feel that they should be in the business of selling pure-bred dogs. As in any other business, they are in it for profit. Buy low and sell as high as the market will bear. Reputable breeders do not sell to pet stores. So where does the stock come from? They buy directly or indirectly from suppliers representing puppy mills.

You might think that the doggie in the window is cute, and even notice that he is pedigreed and registered with the AKC. You may have no intention of breeding him—perhaps you just want a puppy for your children to grow up with. What could go wrong? A simple answer is the dog's temperament. As we mentioned earlier, reputable breeders breed Dachshunds for show. When a dog enters a show ring he must be examined by a judge. If he makes an attempt to bite the judge, he will be immediately excused from the ring, and be disqualified from ever being shown again. If he shies away from the judge, he will be excused, but may be shown again (although his shying away is a pretty good indication that there is a problem with his temperament).

While breeders are obviously concerned with correct conformation and coat, they know that bad temperament will nullify all of the dog's other attributes, so this is of prime consideration when they breed their dogs. It is important to note that a bad temperament may not be recognizable for several months, so every effort should be made to minimize the risk of adopting a dog with this problem at the time of purchase.

Puppy mills are kennels that breed for volume and profit. They are not members of the Dachshund Club of America, nor do they have any interest in breeding for conformation or show. Inbreeding is common, and results in problems in temperament and conformation, as well as assorted congenital problems. Puppies are generally raised with minimal human contact in crowded and unsanitary conditions. We can relate any number and variety of horror stories to you involving various illnesses, structural problems (including paralysis), and premature death. Most puppies at puppy mills are "AKC Registered," although the American Kennel Club makes every effort to investigate and close down kennels that are determined to be puppy mills.

As a potential buyer of a Dachshund, or any other breed for that matter, you should be made aware of the meanings of "AKC Registered" and *pedigree*. To the uninformed, both connote order, acceptance, and perfection. In short, a "seal of approval." Nothing could be further from the truth. In reality, all that "AKC Registered" means is that the dog has been registered with the AKC with regard to his breed, sex, date of birth, sire, dam, breeder, owner, color, and so on. The only prerequisite in order for him to be registered, is that the dog's sire and dam were also registered with the AKC. Don't be fooled by the term "pure-bred." This only means that one Dachshund was bred to another Dachshund. The registered dog could be blind, have three legs, a congenital heart defect, and a preference for chewing on people rather than bones. A pedigree is only a history of the dog's parents, grandparents, and great-grandparents, regardless of the genetic defects that might run in the lineage. If the puppy you purchase from a pet store is not AKC registered, he may not even be a Dachshund.

The AKC's task is as monumental as that of the Drug Enforcement Agency. Out-manned and understaffed, they are fighting an uphill battle,

Six cream longhair Miniature puppies.

"Someday I'll catch a real one!" An eight week old Standard smooth, at about the earliest age for a new home.

and—despite the odds—making progress. If you are in doubt about where to find a Dachshund breeder, you may call the AKC whose headquarters are in New York City. They will refer you to a member of the Dachshund Club of America, who in turn will provide you with a list of names and telephone numbers of breeders in your area. These references will all be members in good standing with the Dachshund Club.

Despite the shortcomings of an AKC Registration, often referred to as a "blue slip," there is one important bit of information that should prompt you into asking further questions about a prospective puppy. If there is a "Ch" immediately preceding the sire and/or dam's name, the parent has met certain requirements in the show ring which have earned him or her the title of, and AKC recognition as, Champion. This generally means that your puppy has been well bred from an excellent representative of the breed, and while there is no guarantee, it is a pretty reliable indication that your source is a good one. This by no means suggests that a reputable breeder must breed to a Champion, so you must go to the next step of asking to see a pedigree. There should be several Ch's in the pedigree. If you see none, a red flag should immediately go up. It is almost a sure thing that a puppy raised in a puppy mill will have no Champions in his pedigree, for the simple reason that a reputable breeder will not breed to any dog without having knowledge of his lineage. Unfortunately, there is no magic formula to help guarantee your selection. These are just some objective clues in helping you to piece together the puzzle.

It's time to make a decision. You have decided on the variety, size, and color of your Dachshund-to-be. You are armed with the objective knowledge, and the right questions to ask. You have been referred to a breeder, and you have arrived at her home or kennel.

It is time for your subjective intuitiveness, combined with additional objective questions and observations, to help you make the right choice.

Standard red smooths at about five weeks.

Don't expect a breeder's home and grounds to look like the White House. A military ordnance proving ground is probably going to be more the rule than the exception, but don't let this deter you. Don't be surprised if your breeder's kennel is no more than a run out of her back door or some crates in the corner of a room. Remember that many reputable breeders may only breed one or two litters a year. The important thing here is to see the kennel and the environment in which the dogs have been raised. If the breeder refuses to let you inside, you may correctly ask yourself, "What do they have to hide?" Use your subjective intuition to form your first opinion. Are the dogs clean and happy? Understanding that you are intruders, are the adult dogs reasonably friendly toward you? Expect them to bark, but look for curiosity rather than fear. Do they wag their tails and appear to show more interest in you as a person rather than a meal? All of these observations are your first indications of the puppies' environment and their ultimate temperament.

We raise all of our litters in the kitchen, where the pups get constant attention from the day that they are born. We have discussed breeding as it relates to personality, and we strongly believe that this is where environment takes over. Even before their eyes and ears open, we pick them up and hold them so that they become used to the human hand. As they grow, we play with them, hug them, and talk to them. It's amazing how much influence this has on them as they develop into adults, and how much easier the transition from our home to another becomes.

You may not be able to determine how and where the puppies were raised. They may be shown to you in a large and open pen either outdoors or in the breeder's home, or they may have been raised in a dark corner of the kennel with very little human contact.

Before attempting to pick up a puppy, quietly observe him for a few minutes. If he sees you, does he come toward you? Does he wag his tail? He may ignore you and appear to be attracted to the breeder. All of these are good

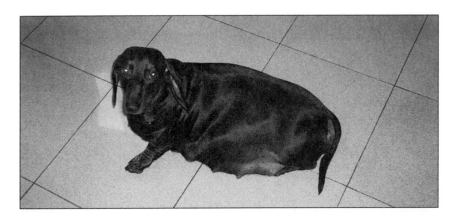

Mama—one week before and two weeks after giving birth.

signs. If the puppies huddle together in a corner and appear frightened, or have their tails between their legs, this could be a sign of a temperament problem or a lack of human attention.

Don't reach into the pen and pick up a puppy. You are a large unknown commodity facing a little Dachshund. Some apprehension will be normal on the puppy's part.

Sit down quietly, and ask the breeder to put the pups on the floor or the ground. You can now begin to talk to them, but don't reach to touch them just yet. They are very inquisitive, and within a short time they should slowly start coming to you with tails wagging. Slowly and gently offer them your hand, and let them smell it.

You are now ready to pick them up—one at a time, of course. At first they may appear somewhat frightened, but this is normal. Pet them gently,

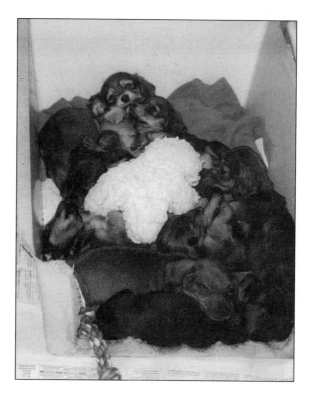

Two litters raised in our kitchen. Note the cleanliness.

and let them lick your face. If you have gotten this far you will be hooked, and you probably are surrounded by well-adjusted and adorable puppies. If possible, ask to see the mother and father. Your puppy will not necessarily grow to look like either, but it will give you some indication of size and general appearance, and most importantly personality and temperament.

Now that the puppies have passed the test, which one do you choose? We can't help you here. The decision is a very personal one and can only be made by you. If you are lucky, the breeder will be charging the same price for all of the puppies, and this price will be within the range that you have established. More likely, they will be different prices depending on their "quality." Quality is a breeder's term, and relates only to a dog's value as a potential show prospect or to his adherence to the Standard as discussed elsewhere in this book. It should not, in any way, be interpreted as labeling the dog negatively with regard to personality or temperament. Often, a puppy may have a "fault" as defined in the Standard. This may be a bad bite which, believe us, in no way impairs their ability to eat, or perhaps a short tail. In the case of a male, the problem may be that he is monorchid, a condition in which only one testicle has descended into the scrotum or the dog was only born with one testicle.

There may be any number of things which may prevent a puppy from being shown, or in the breeder's mind from being bred. Again, we must

Wirehair puppies waiting for a lap.

Miniature smooth Dachshunds—five weeks.

emphasize here that this does not mean that the dog is in any way inferior as far as life expectancy, or has any handicap that might impede his development as a lovable, happy, and well-adjusted animal.

If all you want is a lovable pet, in exchange for a considerably lower price, you may choose to accept a limited registration with the AKC from the breeder. As defined on the reverse side of the registration application, your dog will be registered with the AKC, but any offspring will not be able to be registered. In effect, the breeder is trying to protect her breeding program and the conformation of Dachshunds in general by not passing on "faults" to future generations. Ironically, a puppy mill or a supplier to pet stores would not purchase a puppy under these circumstances, as they would not be able to breed and register future offspring. If you are purchasing a dog for breeding and/or show, the possibilities and options are numerous, and will be discussed in a separate chapter.

Once you have decided that you must have a Dachshund as your pet, we see nothing wrong with acquiring the first dog you fall in love with from a

A Standard wirehair at nine
weeks, ready for a home.

breeder. The initial steps of the selection process for a show dog, however,
might also be considered by you if you have the interest and time to pursue
them. Question your motives for wanting a Dachshund. Does a friend or
relative have one that you particularly like? Is it their appearance, personality, or both that attracted you to them? There are perhaps as many different
"types" of Dachshunds as there are reasons for owning them. Some may be
large boned, and coarse. Others may have a more subtle and refined appearance. There are many dogs that fulfill the requirements of the Standard, and
deservedly earn their championship, yet their general appearance may be
entirely different. The same is of course true of humans—physical attraction,
being subjective in nature, must be left to each individual's preference. Selection is a very personal decision.

If you have seen a particular Dachshund that is attractive to you, try to
find out who bred him. Chances are that the type will be fairly consistent,
and the possibility of finding a similar dog will be very good. If you are un-
sure, try to attend one or more dog shows; if you see a particular dog
that appeals to you, don't be shy. Talk to the owner or handler and find out
who the breeder is. Dog people are generally a friendly lot who will be more
than happy to guide you. Chances are they may have a litter of puppies
at home for sale, or will have one in the near future. If dog shows are inconvenient, the AKC has a Dachshund breed video available at a reasonable
price.

As mentioned previously, a Dachshund Club of America representative
will provide names and telephone numbers of breeders in your area. Call them
and ask questions or visit them at their convenience. If they bark and bite at
you, chances are that their dogs will too. Go on to the next one until you get
the answers you are looking for. As with anything else, research, time, and
patience will ultimately result in finding your perfect dog.

Once you have selected a puppy and agreed upon a price, the breeder
should supply you with a blue slip, signing over the ownership to you. You

Longhair puppies. Their colors can change weekly—our guess is that they became clear reds.

should also request dates and brand names of vaccinations and wormings. Since the earliest we will release puppies is at eight weeks, a booster will be necessary as well as additional wormings.

Ask the breeder for the puppy's feeding schedule and the diet the dog is used to. Either request some food to take with you or purchase some of that brand until your puppy has adjusted to his new environment. If you want to change his diet, do it gradually until the dog is comfortable with his new food.

Congratulations on being the owner of a new Dachshund! Now prepare for your first crisis—the car ride home! Dachshund puppies have a wonderful way of getting carsick. Don't worry, the condition is temporary, and before you know it (or want it) your dog will be in your lap wanting to steer. Be prepared, but not concerned. The condition is normal, and there is no need to return the dog, or make an unplanned trip to the vet.

We do, however, suggest paying the veterinarian a visit at your earliest convenience before making your Dachshund a member of the family. Ask the vet to check him over to insure that he is a healthy animal. This will give you the opportunity, if in fact there is a problem, to return her to the seller before you and your new pup become too attached to each other. Puppies are subject to numerous minor ailments, which are easily and inexpensively correctable, and should not necessarily be reason enough to return them. For instance all puppies, regardless of breed, are born with worms. Keeping them worm free is the ongoing responsibility of the owner. While the conscientious

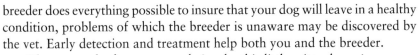

breeder does everything possible to insure that your dog will leave in a healthy condition, problems of which the breeder is unaware may be discovered by the vet. Early detection and treatment help both you and the breeder.

Okay, now the fun starts . . . let's take this little critter home!

A wire puppy at eight weeks. Notice he has not grown whiskers at this age, but the wire coat is beginning to develop on his back.

chapter 3

In-Home Training, Care, and Feeding

Frustration, mutual understanding, anger, respect and, above all, love are but a few of the emotions that you and your Dachshund are about to experience. We're sure you will be able to add to the list. The first few weeks are critical to the successful development of the relationship between you and your dog. Be positive in your approach and enjoy the experience. You will be forever rewarded.

You probably haven't recently installed wall-to-wall carpeting in your home, or graced your dining room with a priceless Persian rug, but regardless of the type of floor covering you own, you are not thinking of your dog's personality development, name, feeding schedule, or beginning to establish a relationship—your first thoughts are how to protect that carpeting. You think to yourself, "I know it's going to happen, it's just a matter of time. Which should I buy first, dog food or rug shampoo?" A crate! Don't walk, run to your nearest supermarket or pet supply store and buy a crate. They are cheap enough, and well worth the price. After your Dachshund is housebroken, the crate can still be used as a bed for traveling either by car or airplane or as a "guest room" when visiting friends. You will want an airline style crate made of plastic and joined at the middle with fasteners that can easily be disassembled for storage. Try to find one with a snap-on water dish, as these are now required by airlines when shipping a dog. The crate should be the smallest one in which your Dachshund will be comfortable. It should be tall enough so that he can stand and long enough so that he can lie down comfortably. Keep in mind that he will generally sleep in a curled position. You will be defeating your purpose if you buy a crate that is too large.

"I'm ready for you, are you ready for me?"

The object is to keep the dog as confined as possible, but not cramped. A bed is not necessary, as simple newspapers and an old towel will work just fine.

A young puppy will make mistakes, either on the floor or in his crate, until he is trained. If he goes on your rugs, you only have yourself to blame. Keep him confined to areas that will not be damaged by mistakes but will, at the same time, provide maximum human contact. We prefer the kitchen, or an uncarpeted den. If you eventually intend to let him go out unattended, then try to keep him in the room where the door is that you will use most frequently to let him go outside.

You should also find either a leather or nylon show leash or lead with a slip fitting which will permit you to adjust the fit around your Dachshund's neck as it grows. A puppy will not walk with you on a lead at first. He must be "broken" similar to a horse, so for that reason we do not recommend a separate collar and leash at the outset, as a Dachshund's long neck and head can easily slip out of a collar.

Separate dishes for food and water will also be necessary. We like the stainless steel ones which can be found in any pet store. Choose a permanent place for the water dish. Dogs should always have (and be able to find) a reliable source of clean and fresh water. The food dish should only be available at feeding time, and should be removed when not in use.

Now that you have all the hardware, the only thing remaining is verbal communication. In the beginning you will need a name and the expressions *"Good Dog!," "Bad Dog!,"* and *"No!"* Any and all forms of communication expressing love and affection will always be gratefully acknowledged and accepted.

Your life together is about to begin. While you both approach the relationship with apprehension and uncertainty, mutual respect and affection are not far off, and you will both be rewarded for your patience.

Now that you have brought your puppy home, he is probably terrified, confused, and still feeling a bit carsick. This is not the time to let your children or other members of the household pounce on your new found joy. Put the puppy on the floor and offer him some water. Have everyone sit on the floor quietly and let the dog come to you. You are now on his level and not as intimidating. The puppy should be very inquisitive and will probably come up to each one of you. He won't linger, but will stay only long enough for a good smell before he finds something else to occupy his attention. Once he realizes that he is in no danger, each of you can begin picking him up. It won't be long before you and the dog will begin feeling comfortable with each other.

Begin using his new name immediately. For our purposes, let's call him Hesa. We'll use Shesa for a female dog. That makes it easier to say, "Shesa good dog" or "Hesa bad dog." Before we begin house training, we should cover the basics of food and water (the latter being the precursor of the former). As mentioned earlier, always have a bowl of fresh water available. Even if your dog doesn't drink that much, change the water two or three times a day, and be consistent by leaving the bowl in the same place—a place that is convenient for both you and the dog.

Assuming that your dog is between eight and ten weeks old, he should be fed three times a day. We do not recommend leaving food on the floor once he has eaten his fill. Pick up the dish, regardless of how much he has eaten, and give him fresh food at the next feeding. Do not be overly concerned if he does not eat any or all of his food; sooner or later he will, when he gets hungry and realizes that he must eat at feeding time or the food will be taken away. Once your dog has reached one year of age, he will only need to be fed once a day. Once a male has reached six months of age, you can generally reduce his food to two meals a day. Often the dog will begin doing this on his own.

We are not going to recommend here how much, or what brand or type of food to feed your puppy. Your breeder can best answer these questions for you, as all puppies are raised differently. Generally speaking, young puppies should be permitted to eat as much as they want following the recommendations provided by the manufacturer of the food, until they reach six months of age. Most name brand foods on the market today are excellent, with constant research and development improving them all the time. You may want to try different brands from time to time to discover which is best for your dog. The important thing to remember is not to let your puppy become overweight as he matures. Being overweight will be bad for his health in general, particularly because it will put too much strain on his long back and short legs. Remember, Dachshunds are con artists and will try anything to get more food than they need. Don't give in and overfeed your dog.

We don't recommend feeding dogs table scraps, and please, no bones which can shatter and become lodged in their throats. Unless it is unappealing to you, you may want to let them lick your plates—as long as most of the food has been removed. Leftover food may be kept and mixed with their regular food at a later time as long as it is not too rich. If your dog does become overweight, he can be put on a diet by cutting back on his food. In a relatively short period of time the weight will begin to come off.

House training is the most frustrating part of making a Dachshund a member of your family. Some take to it faster than others, but with perseverance and patience, all will eventually learn.

Encouragement and praise—not punishment and anger—will speed the accomplishment of your goal. Don't misunderstand us—on occasion a firm hand on an exposed rump may be entirely appropriate, but this should only be necessary as a training tool and not as a means to vent anger. We can think of no circumstance warranting "rubbing the dog's nose in it," and without further discussion, we would discourage anyone from this practice.

The objective here is to praise your dog when he "goes" outside, and not punish him when he "goes" inside. Positive reinforcement is more effective than negative. Don't expect results overnight. Much of the training process requires being in the right place at the right time. Until your dog is trained, he should live in his crate at night, and be in it during the day when you are running errands or if you are going to be in another part of the house for an extended period of time. While sometimes they must (particularly at night when they have been confined for several hours), Dachshunds generally will not make mistakes in their crate—after all, this is where they live, and they generally will refrain from such activity when confined. When you take a Dachshund out of his crate, he should go outdoors immediately and not be given the opportunity to do anything on the floor. Usually Dachshunds will go outside after having been confined. This is the time to praise him. Let him know how happy you are with his performance. If he does nothing outside and shortly thereafter relieves himself inside, pick him up immediately, firmly say, "No!" or "Bad dog!," and take him outside again. Since he has just gone inside, he will not repeat the performance outside, but he will begin to associate outdoors with the proper place to go. One important rule of thumb is to always put your dog outside immediately after he finishes a meal.

During the day, your dog should be free to roam in an area which you have designated. We recommend putting newspapers down, as he will likely relieve himself there rather than on the exposed floor, simply because he was probably raised on papers and is accustomed to using them. While not the object of the exercise, it is better at first to have him use the papers than to associate such activity with the floor, rug, etc. If he errs on the floor, pick him up, scold him, put him first on the papers for a few seconds, and then immediately take him outside.

You really can't be firm with your puppy if you have not caught him in the act. Simply take him outside again. The ideal situation is for you to catch him just as he has gone or is just going. Pick him up and with a persuasive voice say, "No," or "Bad dog," and take him outside.

The ideal way to teach your dog is to take him outdoors every hour or two (experience will tell you how often), so that he doesn't have the chance to go inside. With praise, he will eventually associate doing his thing with being outside. Outdoor frequency will begin to increase, and correspondingly indoor mistakes will decrease. If you feel it necessary, now is the time to increase your firmness with him to include an appropriate pat on his rump. He will now begin to associate outdoors with positive reinforcement and indoors with negative consequences. Which would you choose? Enough said and good luck!

Your Dachshund puppy will need something to chew while cutting teeth as an aid to both keep teeth clean and relieve boredom. Assorted table legs, carpets, and shoes are the least preferable as they are not only expensive to replace, but can result in internal complications for your dog and external pain for your hand as well as his backside. The only safe, natural bones for this purpose are six-inch lengths of round beef shin bones. All others can be broken or splintered and swallowed. Sharp pieces may pierce the intestine or cause a blockage or indigestion. We would recommend that you ask the advice of a pet supply dealer which products are the most beneficial and least dangerous for your Dachshund. New products are always appearing on the market, and a dealer can keep you updated. Rawhide products are among the safest of the chew toys; however, there have been occasional reports of dogs choking on bits of rawhide which have lodged and swollen in their throats. The most recent rage has been smoked pig's ears. Expensive, but effective and nutritious, as long as you can stomach them.

Dog biscuits are the safest things for your dog to chew, but their longevity is severely limited and predictable and may result in the disruption of a carefully balanced diet. The additional cost of a Weight Watchers™ program, and an exercise video may also be a deterrent.

Now that you have a well-adjusted, well-fed, and clean (most of the time) Dachshund, what do you want to do with it? Maybe Obedience or Field Trials. Perhaps you may even want to show your dog. Chances are you just want your Dachshund to be no more than an enjoyable member of the family. As basic as this may sound, there are some decisions that you will have to make. In which parts of the house will he be allowed? Are you going to permit your dog on the furniture or on your bed at night? We personally don't have any problem with these options because Dachshunds do not smell and, as previously mentioned, they don't shed.

Remember, Dachshunds want to be with you every minute. If permitted, they will follow your every move throughout the house and will stop where you do. They have acute memories, so once permitted to do something they like, they will never forget it and will want to repeat the experience whenever possible. They adore riding in cars, and will be excellent companions for you on the way to the market. If left in the car, they will generally curl up on the seat quietly to await your return. Once properly trained, they will go

This longhair puppy doesn't know it's not a Labrador or Golden Retriever.

for 12 hours or more without having to relieve themselves, so beds, cars, and boats are no problem.

Some words of warning to those of you who take your dog with you in the car: as a general rule, we do not recommend leaving your dog, or any animal for that matter, unattended in an enclosed car during the hot summer months. We don't mean just those unbearable humid days, but anytime there is direct sunlight that can turn the inside of your car into an oven. In a matter of minutes, oxygen levels will decrease and temperatures increase at a remarkable rate. Unfortunately many animals have asphyxiated in no more time than it takes to drop off your cleaning and buy a loaf of bread. If you must leave your dog in the car, try to park in the shade and open all windows as far as possible. Our best advice is to leave them at home on hot days.

If you don't want your dog to have the run of the house, or the furniture (in which case we must assume the bed to be out of the question), he will adjust to this environment and it shouldn't effect his personality. He will become accustomed to being confined to his crate when you leave the house or at night. If this is your choice, then he will demand and deserve attention and affection from you whenever you are with him.

Unless your dog is permitted to run loose on your property, he will rarely need to be bathed except in the case of the longhair, which will occasionally need to be combed and bathed to keep him free from mats.

Even if permitted free reign of the outside, bathing should only be necessary when your dog decides to roll in something long deceased, just deceased, or soon to be deceased. If a Dachshund finds a hole in the ground with something living in it, he may dig endlessly and accumulate large quantities of dirt on his paws and legs, requiring a trip to the kitchen sink.

If you live in an area where your Dachshund is free to roam, remember that they are hunters. While your dog will probably stay close to the house, as most Dachshunds do, he may follow his natural instincts, pick up the scent of a bird, squirrel, rabbit, or other animal and take off after it and track it for hours. The only way to prevent this is with an electric fence or by restricting him to a confined enclosed area. Hunting can become a habit not easily broken.

While on this subject, we would be negligent if we did not discuss exercise. If you bought your Dachshund because he was small and would fit nicely into your city apartment thinking that you wouldn't have to worry about exercise, you couldn't have made a worse decision. Dachshunds want and need as much, if not more, exercise as any other breed of dog. Despite their short legs, they love to run, and being hunters they require it.

Although too small to accompany you on your daily jog, they will eagerly keep up with you on long, fast-paced walks and welcome the opportunity to run with you for short distances. When allowed to roam free, they will run for hours, stopping only occasionally for a warm snooze in the sun. It will benefit him both mentally and physically.

Dachshunds are a hardy lot and can go out in all kinds of weather. They love the snow and are amusing to watch frolicking in a foot of new powder with just the tops of their heads and tails visible. But, although they can tolerate all kinds of weather, they should not be made to stay out for long periods in extreme cold or heat.

Another word of caution is in order—we do not recommend permitting your Dachshund to indiscriminately jump on or off your furniture, or force him to run up and down stairs. Whenever possible, carry him when climbing or descending stairs and lift him off a sofa or chair. With a long back and short legs, to or from a sofa can be a long way, and he can injure himself if not careful. We find that putting a stool or intermediate platform in front of your sofa or chair will help alleviate the problem. Some people place a plank from their outdoor deck to the ground (assuming that it's not too high), and their dog uses this instead of the stairs.

With proper care, your Dachshund will be a loving companion for many years. Treat him well—you both deserve it—and neither of you will have any regrets.

"Tucker," one of our Mini wirehairs, at about five months. *Photo courtesy of Shel Segunda Photography.*

chapter 4

Grooming

Whatever your ultimate decision, proper grooming is essential to the well-being of your dog, and it is your responsibility as the owner to see that it is accomplished. Proper grooming of your Dachshund includes more than just an occasional haircut and keeping your dog's coat clean and brushed, but also the care and cleaning of teeth, ears, and nails.

Many of you may choose to have much of what follows done by your veterinarian or a dog grooming shop; however, for more adventurous and cost-conscious souls, we will present you with a comprehensive guide to the complete grooming needs of your Dachshund. With some guidance and practice, anyone should be able to master the art of grooming.

We will begin with basic grooming procedures and then advance to specialized techniques that may require the help of someone more experienced. Some Dachshunds do not like to have their ears and teeth cleaned or their nails trimmed. If your dog reacts this way, or if you have any doubts with regard to your ability to carry out some of these tasks, then we would recommend outside assistance.

If your dog is beginning to look like home plate after a high-scoring baseball game, then it is time for a bath. However, before attempting to bathe, scissor, or trim him, it is essential that you completely brush or comb his coat. Hopefully you have been doing this on a regular basis, as brushing encourages a healthy coat. Brushing stimulates the flow of the natural coat oils and removes tangles in the longhair or wirehair. Brushing also removes any dead hair. In the longs and wires, pay particular attention to the heavily coated areas. Burrs and other assorted tangles in the longs (most prevalent on the ears) do not need to be scissored out. With patience, they can be removed by gently parting the hairs a few at a time at the point of the tangle while intermittently combing or brushing.

Before putting your dog into the bathtub or the sink, place a rubber mat on the bottom to provide sure footing for him. Dachshunds tend to freeze up and stiffen their legs when placed in a sink, either because they don't know what to expect or they do and would prefer not to be there. Test the water temperature before wetting him down. Extremely cold or hot water will be unpleasant for him and will make future baths difficult for both of you. A spray hose attachment will greatly facilitate wetting and rinsing, and a sponge or washcloth will allow you to wash his head, ears and muzzle without getting shampoo in his eyes. Should you accidentally get some shampoo in his eyes, place a drop of mineral oil in each eye to protect against possible irritation.

Any good quality shampoo for people should do the job nicely. If your dog has fleas or a skin problem, your veterinarian or pet supply dealer can recommend an appropriate medicated soap. Be sure to follow the directions. After wetting his coat, apply the shampoo and work it into a rich lather. He will enjoy a brisk massage and it is good for his coat and skin. Rinse and shampoo again. The final rinse cycle should be thorough since any shampoo residue will cause dryness, flaking, and itching.

The first thing your dog will want to do following a bath is shake. Damp dry him first before allowing him to do so, unless you and your surroundings want a bath too. Towel dry him, and then use a hair dryer set on the lowest setting to complete the drying process.

If your dog has developed dry or flaking skin, apply baby or bath oil to his coat, brush it in thoroughly and leave it on for a few hours before bathing. If your Dachshund is a longhair and the coat is either dry, brittle, curly, or wavy, use this same procedure, but follow the bath with a good quality creme rinse. Leave this on the coat for two to three minutes, and then rinse thoroughly. Towel dry your dog. While his coat is still damp, place a dry towel over his back, and pin it securely at the chest and under the belly. Place him in a warm, draft free place until the coat is thoroughly dry, then remove the towel and brush.

Dental hygiene is just as important for your dog as it is for you. While chew toys will help in keeping his teeth clean, periodic brushing is necessary to maintain healthy gums and fresh breath. We suggest using Plax™, a readily available application for people, and cotton balls. A mixture of equal parts of baking soda and salt may also be used. Dip a cotton ball into the Plax™, and rub each tooth. This will loosen the plaque and tartar and facilitate brushing. Recently we have been using a toothbrush with a plastic sleeve that slides over your finger. You can also find them with rubber tips which can be used to massage the gums. If tartar (hardened yellowish-brownish material) does become evident on your dog's teeth, you can use dental scalers to remove it in much the same way as your dentist does. Scalers are available from most large animal supply outlets.

To use the scaler, place it parallel to the tooth on which you are working and at the edge of the gum line. For the upper teeth, draw the scaler down from the gum line to the tip of the tooth using firm pressure. For the lower teeth, draw the scaler up from the gum line to the tip of the tooth. Once all of the teeth have been scaled in this manner, use the Plax™, cotton balls, and toothbrush to remove any remaining bits of matter that you may have missed.

Your dog's ears also need to be cleaned on a regular basis. Should you forget and you see your dog scratching his ears more than usual, or if he rubs his ears along the floor or rug, this is a pretty good indication that he is ready for a cleaning. His ears are sensitive, so you need be careful not to probe too deeply. A cotton-tipped swab or cotton ball dipped in baby or mineral oil will work well for this purpose. You may also use denatured alcohol; however, too much may leave his ears dry.

Regular cleaning will make the job easier each time, and your dog will thank you for it.

Keeping your Dachshund's nails trimmed properly is perhaps the most important, yet least understood, grooming procedure. It is important to keep your dog's nails short, both for his comfort and to prevent his feet from splaying, which allows debris and stones to catch between his pads. For many of you, this process may best be left to your vet, but can easily and safely be done at home if you are so inclined. Whichever you choose, we recommend that your dog's nails be clipped no less frequently than once a month. A vein and a nerve extend about halfway down each nail. If the nail is left to grow without periodic clipping, both will extend further towards the tip of the nail causing bleeding and some discomfort when the nails are clipped to their proper length. Regular clipping will eliminate this problem.

Your Dachshund has a compact foot designed for crossing rough terrain while in pursuit of game. To help keep the foot this way, short nails are a necessity. From a practical standpoint, short nails will neither scratch your floors and furniture, nor catch in clothing, rugs, bedding, and upholstery. We would suggest that you have your vet or someone familiar with clipping nails show you how your first time. She will also be helpful in recommending the best equipment (in addition to a powdered nail clotting material in the event the clipped nail bleeds) for this purpose. Your dog's nail has a very broad base and then a definite point where the nail suddenly begins to taper. It is at this point that the nail should be cut. If you do cut the nail too short and it begins to bleed, take a pinch of the powdered clotting material and press it on the cut end of the nail. The powder is a coagulant and should stop the bleeding quickly. You may have to repeat the procedure, so keep your Dachshund confined, or at least away from rugs and furniture, for no less than an hour to give the nail ample time to permanently clot.

So that you will have a complete picture of what your dog should look like, we will begin with grooming for show, and then give you some helpful hints for grooming your pet. Since grooming procedures are different for each variety of the Dachshund, we will start with the most popular, the smooth, and then go on to the longhair and the wirehair respectively.

Smooth

As the smooth has a short, thick, shiny coat, very little grooming is required. Beginning with the head, use a straight shear with rounded tips to cut the whiskers on the muzzle, over the eyes, on the cheeks, and on the underside of the jaw. These whiskers should be cut very close to the skin. Many breeders leave the whiskers natural and untrimmed. Either way is considered correct and the choice may be left to your discretion. Moving to the neck, if the dog has a particularly thick coat, you may have to scissor the stray hairs on the sides of his neck where the coat growth from the back of the neck joins the growth from the front. You may also have to trim the wispy hairs which may protrude at the point of the breastbone. This may be done with either straight scissors or thinning shears, but cut slowly and carefully so as not to leave a bare spot or sharp line where you have scissored. As for the tail and the feet, if the hair on the underside of the tail is thick and unkempt looking, trim it with scissors or thinning shears to give a sleek tapered look. Trim any hair that may protrude on the underside of the feet, so that the hair is even with the pads. Finally, a light spray of coat dressing oil, or a small amount of baby oil rubbed on your hands and then applied lightly to the coat, will add luster and sheen. If dandruff is evident, wipe the coat down with Listerine™.

That's all there is to grooming your smooth. As far as those helpful pet grooming tips, there are none that relate to the smooth. Aren't you lucky?

Longhair

The longhair is a much longer story. The coat should be rather long and silky, akin to the Irish Setter. Grooming is necessary to enhance this elegance and to accentuate the Dachshund body shape. The most difficult of the longhairs to groom are the reds and chocolates because the undercoat is usually lighter in color. As a result, areas that have been recently scissored are very obvious in the show ring—so reds and chocolates should be groomed about six to eight weeks before the dog is to be shown. Finishing touches and neatening can be done during the last week before a show. The dappled longhair Dachshund presents a unique challenge in that the silver or white hairs of the dappled areas are generally coarser in texture than the other hairs and give a harsher feel when newly cut. It is best to do most of the dappled's grooming six to eight weeks before the show whether they be chocolate, red, or black and tan. Black and tan longhairs, however, can be groomed closer to the date of the show since the coat texture and color are uniform all over the body.

Beginning with the head, cut the whiskers on the muzzle, cheeks, over the eyes, and under the chin using a barber shear with rounded tips. As with the smooth, these whiskers should be cut very close to the skin. Some dogs have longer hairs on their heads which give an unkempt appearance. These

An example of a correctly groomed longhair. *Courtesy Lorene Hogan.*

should be removed by either plucking with the thumb and index finger, or by brushing the coat with a pumice stone in the direction in which it grows.

The coat on the ears should be long and lie flat against the ear. Some dogs, particularly puppies, have excess hair at the area where the ear joins the skull. This gives an overly wide look to the head and detracts from the dog's otherwise elegant appearance. This hair may be plucked or removed with a thinning shear. When using a thinning shear, place the blades under the coat near the top of the ear and cut only once or twice. Comb the cut area to determine whether that area should be thinned again. Be careful, as aggressive cutting can result in a bald spot. Continue to cut, comb, and evaluate until you have the desired effect. The hair on the inside of the ear at the cheek area and around to the small flap on the inside back of the ear should be cut very close, permitting the ear to lie flatter against the head and to outline the ear against the neck.

The hair on the neck of the longhair should be long, lean, and taper into the shoulder area in a very elegant manner. Heavy coat growth tends to make the neck appear too short. Thinning shears should be used from the back of the jaw down the front of the neck to a point just above the point of the breastbone. Hold the dog's head up with one hand, and place the thinning shears under the coat against the skin and in line with the coat growth (never across the direction of the coat growth). Cut once or twice, then comb it to see if you need to cut again. Thin the hair from the underside of the jaw downward into a long, full coat beginning just above the breastbone. Thin the total neck area to the point where the coat growth coming from the back of the neck joins the hair on the front of the neck on each side.

To groom the back of the neck, we prefer to begin with a stripping knife. This gem of a tool has a very fine serrated edge, and when used like a comb, will remove an amazing amount of dead hair and undercoat without affecting the longer outer coat. Because of the very fine edge on this tool, it must be used slowly with the skin kept taut in the area in which you are grooming. If you are not careful, the tiny teeth may catch in a small fold of skin.

Comb with the stripping knife until no more hair falls out. If the neck area still looks too thick, use the thinning shears to achieve a sleek, elegant, lean look. Be sure to cut, comb, and evaluate. The back of the neck should taper and blend into the shoulder area.

The main body is best groomed again using the stripping knife in a combing motion down the length of the body and down the sides to remove dead hair and undercoat. The body coat should lie flat and taper into a flowing coat on the sides and underside of the body. Thinning shears can be used judiciously to enhance the topline and sleekness.

Moving to the legs—the hair behind the front legs should form a pronounced feather. Heavy growth on the front legs can give the appearance that the elbows are pointing outward. To correct this, use the thinning shears on the outer sides of the front legs, particularly at the elbow area. This will give a close fitting look to the legs. The long hair on the back of the front legs should be combed toward the back of the body. If the coat is too profuse and tends to protrude towards the sides, use thinning shears until you are able to comb it back. It is also helpful to frequently dampen this hair before combing it back, in order to train the direction of the hair growth.

The hair on the back of the thighs should also be long and full, but not protruding outward to the side of the back legs. Use the thinning shears to blend this coat into the upper thigh area.

Cut the hair on the bottom of the feet so that it is even with the pads. With the foot placed securely on a firm surface, trim the hair using a straight scissor. The desired look is a rounded compact foot. You may have to trim the hair on the top of the foot—in the area of the nails— to remove the wispy hairs which stick up over the nails. Do not cut the hair in an outline around the nails; rather, cut so as to blend this hair to a fully coated, round appearance.

The coat of the longhaired Dachshund should reach its greatest length on the underside of the tail; therefore, little is done to the tail other than combing and brushing it to maintain its condition.

If you do not already own a longhair, we hope that the foregoing will not discourage you. Following are some helpful and easy tips for keeping your dog a beautiful and well-groomed pet.

All you really need to do is to periodically comb the back of your dog's neck and body with the stripping blade on a somewhat regular basis. We will leave the frequency up to you, as appearance can be somewhat subjective. Diligent care, however, will remove dead hair and undercoat and keep the coat in good condition, not to mention the added advantage of not having to frequently vacuum your furniture. We would also recommend using a thinning shear on the sides of the neck, where the coat growth from the back of the neck joins the front. Scissoring the hair on the bottom of the feet even with the pads will also prevent dirt and debris from accumulating. You also need to keep the ear hair trimmed. Comb the coat using a flea comb, which will remove the dead hair.

Regular (but not overly frequent) bathing followed by a creme rinse and lots of brushing and combing will keep your dog's coat in good, shining condition.

Wirehair

Keeping your wirehaired Dachshund perfectly groomed generally takes more time and knowledge than the other two varieties, however wires do not shed to the extent of longhairs, and therefore frequent grooming is not necessary. In general, show grooming requires a combination of plucking and/ or stripping, whereas pet grooming is easily achieved with an electric clipper. Many pet owners prefer a longer, ungroomed appearance on their wires, but they are such beautiful animals that our preference is to keep their coat at the proper length (approximately one inch when laying flat) with periodic grooming.

With the exception of the jaw, eyebrows, and ears, the whole body of the wirehaired Dachshund is covered with a perfectly uniform, tight, short, thick, rough coat, and an undercoat of finer, shorter hair, which is distributed between the coarser hairs (like the coat of the German wirehaired Pointer). The dog should have a beard on his chin and the eyebrows should be bushy. The hair on the ears is shorter than on the body, but conforms to the rest of the coat. The general arrangement of the hair should be such that when seen from a distance, the wirehaired Dachshund will resemble the smooth. As paraphrased from the Dachshund Standard, this briefly describes the challenge in grooming the wirehair by enhancing the Dachshund shape and emphasizing the wire characteristics.

There are basically three methods to correctly groom the wirehair for show—namely plucking, stripping, and a combination of both. Clippering, while preferred by many for grooming a pet, is never done as preparation for the show ring. While plucking can be a tedious process, periodic and regular use of this technique by the pet owner can be both time and cost effective.

Plucking consists of using the thumb and index finger to literally pluck or pull out the longer coat hairs. Even though we would not permit it to be done to us unless we were under general anesthesia, it in no way causes pain or discomfort to your wirehair.

Stripping is done with a stripping knife (there are many designs and models available, so you should find one which is comfortable for you to use). Stripping is accomplished by placing the knife against the coat, catching a small amount of hair against the blade with your thumb, and pulling the longer hairs from the coat. The hair should be pulled, always in the direction of coat growth, with quick, jerking motions.

When you plan to remove a great deal of the coat—referred to as taking the coat down—the major part of the work should be done eight to twelve weeks before the date of the show. The rate of growth will differ from dog to dog, so

Drawing by Gina Leone.

you might have to experiment to determine the best time schedule for your dog. If he is a pet, your dog should be clippered in lieu of plucking or stripping on about the same schedule, but perhaps it can be deferred a bit longer.

Once the coat is at the desired length, it can be maintained by stripping or plucking the longer hairs weekly. This will remove any dead hair, and allow for steady growth of new hair. This procedure is known as rotating the coat.

The head should be stripped or plucked from just behind the eyebrows, over the top of the skull, and down into the neck area; the cheek area from the outer corner of the eye to the corner of the lip; and between the eyes as well. Stray hair at the inner corner of the eye should be removed, and the eyebrows should be longer at the inside corner of the eye tapering to the outside corner, where they are flush with the skull structure. The eyebrows should be short enough to allow the eyes to see—and readily *be* seen.

The overall head structure should be uniformly tapered, and it may be necessary to thin out the dog's beard to achieve this look. It is also possible

Impeccably groomed, these stud dogs (photo taken circa 1970) were the foundation for today's wire-hairs.

to remove some of the coat from the center of his under jaw to allow the beard to lie closer against the muzzle.

The longer hairs should be removed from the outside and underside of the ears. This will leave a very short undercoat on the ear. Usually this hair only needs to be removed once or twice, as it does not tend to grow back. The hair on the inside of the ear, where the ear joins the cheek, should be scissored very close to the skin to allow the ear to lie flat against the cheek.

The longer hairs on the neck should be stripped or plucked under the chin and down the throat to the breastbone, along the sides of the neck, and on the back of the neck, blending into the shoulder area.

The body coat should be kept about 1/2–3/4 inch in length, which is a little longer than his head and neck. Stripping or plucking should begin at the top of the head, following down the neck, along the topline and sides, back to his tail. The underside should be stripped or plucked to conform to the rest of his body. You do not want to leave a great length of coat here, as it will wind up looking like a skirt. If your dog does not have a deep chest, groom the coat on the underside of his body, so that the chest area looks slightly longer, and taper it up into the loin area. His tail should be plucked or stripped to give an even tapered appearance. Since the underside of the tail may be sensitive, you may wish to use thinning shears on this area. When using any type of scissor, always cut with the growth of the hair, never against it. Be sure to cut the hairs around the anus for a neat appearance, to conform with the rest of the grooming.

The hair on his legs should conform to his body coat, but may be just a bit longer. Judiciously pluck or strip the longer hairs to enhance the full wire coat growth.

Use straight scissors to trim the hair on the bottom of the feet, even with the pads. With his foot placed securely on a flat surface, use a straight scissor to trim the hair around his foot. The desired effect is again one of a rounded, compact foot.

While pet grooming of the wire is a bit more complicated than the smooth or longhair, you can easily accomplish it with some practice and a good clipper set. Clippers come with separate blades, all of which are designed to uniformly cut the coat at the same length. You will need a #10 blade for the head, underside of the neck, and ears, and either a #5 (leaves hair $\frac{1}{2}$ inch long) or a #7 (leaves hair $\frac{1}{4}$ inch long) for the back of the neck, the body, and tail.

The blade you choose depends upon your preference, but the shorter the coat, the fewer times you will have to groom your dog. Clippering is a time-saving method of keeping him neat, and generally conforming to the desired appearance of the wirehaired Dachshund; however, in most instances you will not be able to maintain the harsh coat texture by doing so. Clippering should follow the same pattern as outlined for show grooming.

If you really want to "cheat," use only the #10 blade if you are not going to show your dog. This will make his coat very short and will only have to be repeated every eight weeks. We do it all the time, but please, leave his beard and eyebrows and just trim as necessary.

While you may decide to have your Dachshund groomed professionally, we can assure you that with a little patience you can accomplish all of these procedures with confidence. Besides being fun, it is cost effective.

Remember, grooming helps your dog maintain a proper appearance, good comfort, and good health. It is a responsibility not to be taken lightly.

chapter 5

Health and Medical Considerations

No one likes to think about the possibility of his Dachshund needing medical attention. In reality, however, every dog—Dachshunds included—will need medical attention from time to time. You must constantly be aware of your dog's state of health through observation. Through a regular program of care and periodic check-ups, learn how to identify and anticipate potential problems before they become serious.

We cannot provide you with a comprehensive medical manual of diagnosis, prognosis, treatment, and care for you dog's illnesses. Medical problems that occur in all dogs are as numerous and varied as those associated with humans. We will make no attempt to elaborate on a subject best left to a those trained in such matters.

What we will attempt to do is offer a first-aid approach from our own experiences, which should help you recognize and respond to common illnesses associated with Dachshunds. We will also offer some of our remedies for minor ailments and tips on preventive medicine that have worked for us. Needless to say, if you have questions on anything covered herein—or on any other medical problem for that matter—be sure to consult your vet.

When you bought your dog, you should have received a health record indicating dates of inoculations and wormings, along with the brand names and quantities of medications administered. We also hope you have taken our advice and had him examined by a veterinarian (if you haven't taken this first step, return to "GO" and start all over again).

As previously mentioned, most puppies are infested with roundworms. The presence of worms should not be considered a bad reflection on the breeder. At eight weeks, your puppy should have been wormed at least twice (at two to three, and five to six weeks respectively). Available worming medicines are far less toxic to dogs today than they were several years ago, so more frequent wormings are common. While the roundworm is by far the most prevalent in young dogs, hookworms, whipworms, tapeworms, and threadworms may also be present. Before attempting to worm your Dachshund, have your vet take a stool sample, then proceed with the brand, dosage, and frequency recommended. Worms are passed in the feces which should be disposed of properly in order to help prevent transmission to other animals.

Many adult dogs may not require additional wormings, but we suggest that you have your dog checked annually at the very least—preferably semiannually. Proceed with worming when necessary.

Heartworm must be addressed separately. Although diagnosis and treatments have become more reliable in recent years, if left untreated the condition will surely be fatal. The larvae of this parasite are transmitted by infected mosquitoes and deposited onto the dog's skin. It penetrates the skin and makes its way into the bloodstream. After undergoing several metamorphoses, it develops into a mature worm between four to twelve inches in length, which establishes residence in the heart. If your dog resides in the city, he has less of a chance of being exposed to mosquitoes than a country dog. But remember, it only takes one bite. While treatable, the disease is best to be avoided. We give each of our Dachshunds a pill once a month. Again, consult your vet, and follow his directions as to the recommended program for your dog.

While nursing on their mother's milk, puppies are immune to many serious diseases. Once weaned, this immunity disappears rapidly. For this reason, your dog should be vaccinated for a combination of viruses including distemper, hepatitis, leptospirosis, and parvo before he is released to you. After approximately sixteen weeks, your vet will administer a booster. Each vet might suggest different schedules, but generally the vaccination will be repeated at one year of age and a booster administered once each year thereafter. If you live in an apartment and walk your dog on a lead, his chances of coming in contact with rabies are minimal. However, dog licensing as well as domestic and international travel require rabies vaccinations. As a precaution, we would recommend, as we are sure your vet will, that this be done.

Your Dachshund will undoubtedly be afflicted with one of two eating disorders: eating too little (which seems to be more prevalent in the Miniatures), or eating too much (which is the more likely of the two scenarios). Rarely will any Dachshund be satisfied with a normally proportioned meal. As previously mentioned, Dachshunds have excellent memories, are stubborn, and will do whatever is necessary to get their way. It will always be you against him, and you must establish that you have the upper hand at the outset.

Surprisingly, some Dachshunds eat to live, rather than the opposite. Many owners, in an effort to get them to eat, will stray from a proper well-balanced diet to bribery in the form of fresh meat. This is precisely what the dog has in mind, and once introduced to gourmet cuisine, he may never return to normal eating habits. This may only contribute to eventual health problems. Dachshunds will never starve to death unless, of course, they are not offered food. A Dachshund may go for days eating little or no food, holding out for that medium-rare filet with bernaise sauce, believing that his resolve will overcome yours. Trust us—don't fall for it. Offer him normal fresh food each day. After a reasonable period of time remove the dish. Repeat the procedure daily until he eventually succumbs. This is not cruel, but crucial for a long and healthy life. If he continues her refusal to eat, or if severe weight loss is evident, this may be a sign of a more serious problem and your vet should be consulted. He may suggest a change in diet to include any one of a number of prescription foods available.

Where one dog may refuse to eat, another may constantly be craving food. Each dog is an individual with his own nutritional needs. One might be "roly-poly" and another a "rack of bones," though they eat the same amount of food. Through trial and error, you must find the proper balance for your dog. Overfeeding and dramatic increases in protein can result in problems in the urinary tract, lower the resistance to viral and bacterial infections, impair cardiac functions, increase susceptibility to skin conditions, put greater demands on your dog's spine, and is also associated with reproductive problems and shortened life-span.

Simply stated, if you permit your dog to remain overweight, he will die prematurely. If we haven't convinced you, and you insist on feeling sorry for him, at least cut down on the size of your dog's meal, and supplement it with treats such as biscuits, small amounts of table scraps and plate licking—all, of course, in moderation. Should he commandeer your child's peanut butter sandwich in a sneak attack, simply withhold his normal meal for that day. If he gains unnecessary weight, simply reduce the amount of his daily meal until he returns to normal. While we certainly would not recommend it on a steady basis, or as a means of forced diet, inadvertent fasting for a day will have no ill effects on your dog.

Bugs—mosquitoes, fleas, mites, ticks, flies, bees, and other creepy crawly things that go bump in the night . . . country living is wonderful for us, but it can be shear misery for Dachshunds if they are not kept in check. Humans do not tread the ground (where so many of these pests live) on all fours. We also have hands to swat them and applications to repel them. We bathe daily and are usually clothed. Dachshunds, on the other hand, are close to the ground, love to hunt, enjoy digging and rolling, and, in general, can be magnets for unwanted critters. You might periodically spray your property with insecticides to control fleas and ticks, but these are only marginally effective. Regular checks of your dogs, and occasional medicated baths are still required.

Bugs are an uncomfortable and inconvenient nuisance for you and your Dachshund. Ordinarily, serious problems will not arise unless their presence is left unattended. During the summer months, we suggest that you go over your dog on a daily basis. Look in his ears, through his coat, on his stomach, and particularly around his genitals and under his tail. Constant ear scratching may be a sign of ear mites, and scratching or biting around his rear may be indicative of fleas.

Normally, there are no behavioral changes or otherwise obvious signs of ticks, and often you will not see them. Discovery comes with your fingers, when you run your hand through the coat.

Two varieties of mites are of concern to dog owners—those that infest the ears and those that live in the skin. They can't be seen with the naked eye. Ear mites live in the ear canals and feed on the skin of the inner ear. They do not appear to be painful to your Dachshund, but they cause intense itching and, if left untreated, will cause infection. The ears should be cleaned in the usual fashion, and a medicine should be applied as prescribed by your vet. As is the case of all parasites, several treatments will probably be necessary to rid the area not only of the pests, but of the eggs left behind.

The mites that live on and lay their eggs under the skin cause a skin disease known as *mange*, used generically here as there is more than one variety. It can be highly contagious and may therefore appear on your puppy sometime after you bring him home. It also causes itching and is identifiable by scabbing and loss of hair in the infected area. It is treatable by a succession of medicated baths as recommended by your vet. Your dog will not experience any lasting effects. Again, this is not necessarily the sign of an unclean kennel. Every breeder we know has experienced the problem from time to time.

The female blood tick, as its name suggests, lives on your dog's blood. If just the idea bothers you, then wait until you remove your first one. If you live in the country, you will inevitably have to contend with ticks, so get used to it! As ghastly as they sound at first, they soon become only a nuisance, rarely causing lasting problems or infections. Before they decide to chomp down on their first meal, they are flat, and about the size of a match tip. Once they become firmly entrenched, they fill with blood and swell to the size of a pea. This is generally when you will first discover them. Some people recommend killing them by applying nail polish or alcohol before removal—this works, but it is not necessary.

Since the tick's head will be firmly embedded in the skin, it is important to try to remove it while intact and not leave all or some of the head behind. To accomplish this, grasp the tick with the nails of your thumb and index finger, getting as close to the skin as possible. Once firmly grasped, pull the tick with a slow, steady motion, carefully avoiding any sudden jerks. Tweezers can also be an effective tool for achieving the same result. You may wish to cleanse the area with some alcohol, but an infection will rarely result. Unless permitted to become infested, your Dachshund will not display any noticeable discomfort from the presence of ticks.

The second, and potentially more dangerous, variety is the deer tick, which was first identified in the northeastern United States and has rapidly spread to other parts of the country. If not treated properly, the resultant Lyme disease may cause serious cardiovascular, muscular, and arthritic problems in both dogs and humans. The initial problem, other than knowing if a particular tick is carrying the disease, is in its identification. The deer tick is tiny. About the size of the point of a newly sharpened pencil, we have found them on our dog's eyelids, but to discover them anywhere else would be near impossible. With early diagnosis, the disease can be treated easily and effectively, so it is important that you see your vet whenever the symptoms become evident.

Recognizing symptoms is the second problem. The one dog we had that contracted Lyme disease experienced loss of appetite, slept continuously, and exhibited listless behavior. If your Dachshund experiences any of these symptoms, your vet can diagnose the disease through blood tests and treat it easily with oral medications. Since only infected deer ticks will carry the disease, the mere presence of one on your dog will not mean that the disease is imminent. Watch him carefully for behavioral changes over the next few weeks before rushing off to your vet.

Fleas may be the largest parasitic problem you will encounter—and they are not associated exclusively with country living. Not only will your dog suffer from constant bites and incessant itching but, if not given immediate attention, you will too. If you think you may have flea problems, a good first step is to purchase a flea collar. Your dog should wear this during the spring, summer, and autumn months. While not a cure-all, it will act as a deterrent. Fleas eat and reproduce on your dog, but their eggs don't need to incubate there. In other words, they will fall off, develop, and live in carpets, furniture, and bedding. Having indiscriminate palates, they will seek out not only your dog, but you too!

Aside from your dog's itching, the fleas' presence is identifiable from the presence of black and white specks which can be found anywhere on your dog, but are most commonly found in warm, moist areas such as their stomachs, groins, and tails. These specks are their eggs and droppings.

Although easily seen with the naked eye, fleas themselves are elusive and will rapidly disappear into the coat. They are very quick and can "leap tall buildings in a single bound." Catching and killing them is nearly impossible. An aggressive plan of attack is necessary when seeking out and destroying the eggs. In addition to the succession of insecticide dips which will be required for your dog, you will also need to eliminate them from carpets and furniture through the use of sprays and dusting powders. In extreme cases, a professional exterminator may be required.

Fleas are also an intermediate host for tapeworm. Have your vet check your dog for this probability.

In addition to these parasites, a number of biting flies will appear during different seasons of the year. Most of these will prove only to irritate your dog, leaving welts or exposed areas on the skin. Any number of fly and mosquito repellents are available as sprays and lotions. Be careful not to get any in the dog's eyes, ears, or mouth. A vast number of prescription ointments for treating minor infections and skin irritations caused by insect bites are available through your vet. We would highly recommend an antibiotic ointment called Panolog™. It is effective for all sorts of skin irritations. It is to be used only in the treatment of cats and dogs.

Though problems like parasites are generic to all breeds, some medical problems happen to be more prevalent in the Dachshund. We will discuss two of these, but do not want to leave the impression that sooner or later your dog will necessarily succumb to one or both of these. We mention them only because we have had some experience with both over many years of breeding and owning Dachshunds. The odds are in your favor that your dog will never have either problem.

If you are prone to gagging while brushing your teeth, feel faint when having a blood test, or refuse to smell a carton of milk to see if it has soured, then you best leave the following to your vet or a professional grooming parlor. There are two glands or sacs located on either side and towards the bottom of the anus. It is thought that these anal glands exist for territorial marking, or identification, which may account for dogs greeting each other by mutually sniffing rears. The glands are routinely emptied when the dog defecates, but sudden fear or distress may also make them active. In some instances, particularly in small dogs, they do not empty on their own and may become impacted and abscessed. This can be very painful for your Dachshund and will require veterinary attention. Most grooming parlors will routinely empty these glands while bathing, but occasionally they may emit an unpleasant odor or become enlarged and so you have the privileged option of doing it yourself. Since the resultant odor is unpleasant, the procedure is best done in a sink with running water ready.

To empty the glands, stand your dog on a firm surface with the hindquarters toward you. Hold the tail up with one hand, and with the other place a piece of cotton, a gauze pad, or several tissues over the rectal area. With your thumb and forefinger, press slightly inward on either side of the rectal opening. Gradually squeeze your fingers together toward the opening and outward away from the dog's body. Repeat the procedure until no more fluid is emitted, followed by a thorough bathing of the area. Your dog should not experience pain or discomfort from this procedure and after a while, neither will you.

The second problem to be addressed is "hot spots." A hot spot is a painful, open sore on your dog resulting from a bacterial infection. Generally associated with heavy coated breeds, we have found the condition to be most prevalent in the longhairs, but the smooth and wire are not immune. Characterized by a circular, warm, swollen patch of skin, the area can expand rapidly causing pain, infection, and loss of hair. We would recommend that you consult your vet for treatment, but it doesn't end there. The area is normally bathed with a surgical soap or diluted hydrogen peroxide. This is followed by an application of sulfadene and Panolog™. Treatment should be repeated several times a day, and every effort should be made to restrain your dog from licking or rubbing the area. Clean ears, anal glands, and absence of fleas are important considerations in the prevention of this condition.

Each breed of dog seems to have at least one disease that affects it disproportionately more than others. Dachshunds are no exception. The incidence of Canine Disc Disease in Dachshunds is twice that of all other breeds combined. While the causes are not completely known, it is thought to be the result of several factors including heredity, breeding, environment, and the physical structure of the breed. In layman's terms, a ruptured or herniated disc occurs, resulting in the pinching of the spinal cord or nerve roots resulting in pain, weakness, lameness, and in some instances complete paralysis of the rear legs. Eighty percent of disc disease occurs in the lower back and the remainder in the neck. Symptoms include the hunching-up of the back, panting, weakness or wobbling when walking, and general pain. If the problem is in the neck area, the dog will cry when patted on the head and will hold his neck in a rigid position. The prognosis varies by case, as discs will affect each dog differently.

In some cases, confinement and rest are successful, and in others surgery may be required. Often, paralysis will result in complications affecting the urinary functions and causing bladder infections. Often, the dog may eventually have to be put to sleep.

Before you run off to find another breed, we can assure you that we have not experienced the problem with any of our dogs in over fifteen years. Reputable breeders will knowingly not breed any dogs or their progeny if they are aware of past or present evidence of disc problems. This is one of the reasons that we stress again the importance of purchasing your Dachshund from a reputable breeder. We would also urge you again not to permit your dog to jump on or off of furniture or to climb stairs when not necessary. Short legs will not have the shock absorbing capabilities of a dog with longer legs—and the long back suspended between the front and rear shoulders has less support than other breeds, making the Dachshund more susceptible to back injuries. If your Dachshund falls in love with a particular piece of furniture, find a fabric-covered stool which can serve as an intermediate step. Some Dachshunds will sit up on their hind legs with no coaxing from you—and there is little you will be able to do about it. But please, don't teach or encourage this practice.

Many over-the-counter drugs commonly used by people may also be administered, in moderation and reduced dosages, to dogs. In older dogs, aspirin may be used for pain and arthritis. Products such as Kaopectate™ and Pepto Bismol™ are effective for mild cases of diarrhea, as are mineral oil or Milk of Magnesia™ for constipation. Again it is best to consult your vet for appropriate dosage and frequency.

From time to time you will be required to administer medication in the form of pills. We can guarantee that your Dachshund will not voluntarily swallow a pill. If you simply put it in her mouth, you will find it later somewhere on the floor. If you hide it in her food, it will be all that remains in the bowl. Hand-feeding a hamburger with the pill carefully concealed will often be successful, but the only sure method is to open the mouth, place the pill far back on the tongue and partially down the throat, even to the point of gagging if necessary. Close and hold the dog's mouth shut. With his head back, gently message the throat until the pill is swallowed. Recheck the mouth to insure that it has not been cleverly concealed in the cheeks or under the tongue.

Apart from the health risks that are out of your hands, such as illness, there are a number of safety hazards that you can safeguard your dog against. A dog may chew on any number of things that are either toxic or otherwise dangerous. Electrical cords, and baseboards covered with leaded paint are only two examples. While primarily carnivorous, Dachshunds will chew on plants which may cause rashes or, more seriously, abdominal discomfort. Common household plants such as chrysanthemums, poinsettias, Boston ivy, and azaleas are only a few problem-causing plants. When left alone, either confine your dog or remove tempting items that he might consider an attractive diversion. Think of yourself as a type of seeing eye person for a blind dog.

chapter 6

Breed Standard

The Breed Standard is a description of the ideal Dachshund. It is in a constant state of evolution, and periodic changes may be made to it as approved by the membership of the Dachshund Club of America, Inc. It is submitted to, and becomes accepted by, the American Kennel Club as the official Standard. The Standard as presented here was approved April 7, 1992 and became effective May 27, 1992.

Prior to a detailed presentation of the Standard, the following brief description of the Dachshund Club of America is appropriate.

- The Dachshund Club of America, Inc., a member of the American Kennel Club since 1895, has more than 1500 members and 51 active DCA Regional Specialty Clubs across the United States.

- DCA is financially supportive of medical research on behalf of the Dachshund.

- Bronze plaques, medallions and gold-plated pins are provided by DCA as prizes at the Parent Club Shows, Regional Specialties, as well as Field and Obedience Trials. Certificates are awarded to Dachshunds who perform meritoriously in conformation, Obedience, and Field Work.

- A DCA Newsletter is published quarterly for the membership providing a forum for informative articles, interviews and kennel advertising.

Just as there is a Standard for the breed, there is an expected Standard for membership in the DCA which is expressed in the following code of ethics:

First in the Hound Group 105 times and 26 Best in Shows, Ch. Starbarrack Halachite ("Ben") is shown winning First in Group at the 1997 Westminster Kennel Club Show. Beautifully presented by longtime Dachshund handler Robert Fowler. *Photo: Ashbey Photo.*

1. To abide by and uphold the principals of the by-laws of the Dachshund Club of America, Inc. and the American Kennel Club.

2. To devote ourselves to the betterment of the breed.

3. To keep our dogs in healthy condition and in a healthy environment.

4. Cover by written agreement all stud service terms and keep accurate written records of matings, births, registration, and so forth.

5. Refrain from any deceptive or erroneous advertising.

6. Cover, in writing, all bills of sale with detailed accuracy.

7. Urge the spaying or neutering of bitches or dogs not desirable for breeding.

8. Supply no animals to pet shops, commercial brokers or dealers, raffles, or similar projects.

9. Provide each purchaser of a dog with:
   - A three generation pedigree.
   - A complete medical record.
   - Details on proper feeding and care.

Excellent specimens bred nearly 40 years ago.

OFFICIAL AKC STANDARD OF THE DACHSHUND

General Appearance—Low to ground, long in body and short of leg with robust muscular development, the skin is elastic and pliable without excessive wrinkling. Appearing neither crippled, awkward, nor cramped in his capacity for movement, the Dachshund is well-balanced with bold and confident head carriage and intelligent, alert facial expression. His hunting spirit, good nose, loud tongue and distinctive build make him well-suited for below-ground work and for beating the bush. His keen nose gives him an advantage over most other breeds for trailing. Note: Inasmuch as the Dachshund is a hunting dog, scars from honorable wounds shall not be considered a fault.

Size, Proportion, Substance—Bred and shown in two sizes, Standard and Miniature, Miniatures are not a separate classification but compete in a class division for "11 pounds and under at twelve months of age and older." Weight of the Standard size is usually between sixteen and thirty-two pounds.

Head—Viewed from above or from the side, the head tapers uniformly to the tip of the nose. The eyes are of medium size, almond-shaped and dark-rimmed, with an energetic, pleasant expression; not piercing; very dark in color. The bridge bones over the eyes are strongly prominent. Wall eyes, except in the case of dappled dogs, are a serious fault. The ears are set near the top of the head, not too far forward, of moderate length, rounded, not narrow, pointed, or folded. Their carriage, when animated, is with the forward edge just touching the cheek so that the ears frame the face. The skull is slightly arched, neither too broad nor too narrow, and slopes gradually with little perceptible stop into the finely-formed, slightly arched muzzle. Black is the preferred color of the nose. Lips are tightly stretched, well covering the lower jaw. Nostrils well open. Jaws opening wide and hinged well back of the eyes, with strongly developed bones and teeth. Teeth—Powerful canine teeth; teeth fit closely together in a scissors bite. An even bite is a minor fault. Any other deviation is a serious fault.

Neck—Long, muscular, clean-cut, without dewlap, slightly arched in the nape, flowing gracefully into the shoulders.

Trunk—The trunk is long and fully muscled. When viewed in profile, the back lies in the straightest possible line between the withers and the short, very slightly arched loin. A body that hangs loosely between the shoulders is a serious fault. Abdomen—Slightly drawn up.

Forequarters—For effective underground work, the front must be strong, deep, long and cleanly muscled. Forequarters in detail:
    Chest—The breastbone is strongly prominent in front so that on either side a depression or dimple appears. When viewed from the front, the thorax appears oval and extends downward to the midpoint of the forearm. The enclosing structure of well-sprung ribs appears full and oval to allow, by its ample capacity, complete development of heart and lungs. The keel merges gradually into the line of the abdomen and extends well beyond the front legs. Viewed in profile, the lowest point of the breast line is covered by the front leg.

Shoulder Blades—Long, broad, well-laid back and firmly placed upon the fully developed thorax, closely fitted at the withers, furnished with hard yet pliable muscles.

Upper Arm—Ideally the same length as the shoulder blade and at right angles to the latter, strong of bone and hard of muscle, lying close to the ribs, with elbows close to the body, yet capable of free movement.

Forearm—Short; supplied with hard yet pliable muscles on the front and outside, with tightly stretched tendons on the inside and at the back, slightly curved inwards. The joints between the forearms and the feet (wrists) are closer together than the shoulder joints, so that the front does not appear absolutely straight. Knuckling over is a disqualifying fault.

Feet—Front paws are full, tight, compact, with well-arched toes and tough, thick pads. They may be equally inclined a trifle outward. There are five toes, four in use, close together with a pronounced arch and strong, short nails. Front dewclaws may be removed.

Hindquarters—Strong and cleanly muscled. The pelvis, the thigh, the second thigh, and the metatarsus are ideally the same length and form a series of right angles. From the rear, the thighs are strong and powerful. The legs turn neither in nor out.

Metatarsus—Short and strong, perpendicular to the second thigh bone. When viewed from behind, they are upright and parallel.

Feet—Hind Paws—Smaller than the front paws with four compactly closed and arched toes with tough, thick pads. The entire foot points straight ahead and is balanced equally on the ball and not merely on the toes. Rear dewclaws should be removed.

Croup—Long, rounded and full, sinking slightly towards the tail.

Tail—Set in continuation of the spine, extending without kinks, twists, or pronounced curvature, and not carried too gaily.

Gait—Fluid and smooth. Forelegs reach well forward, without much lift, in unison with the driving action of hind legs. The correct shoulder assembly and well-fitted elbows allow the long, free stride in front. Viewed from the front, the legs do not move in exact parallel planes, but incline slightly inward to compensate for shortness of leg and width of chest. Hind legs drive on a line with the forelegs, with hocks (metatarsus) turning neither in nor out. The propulsion of the hind leg depends on the dog's ability to carry the hind leg to complete extension. Viewed in profile, the forward reach of the hind leg equals the rear extension. The thrust of correct movement is seen when the rear pads are clearly exposed during rear extension. Feet must travel parallel to the line of motion with no tendency to swing out, cross over, or interfere with each other. Short, choppy movement, rolling or high-stepping gait, close or overly wide coming or going are incorrect. The Dachshund must have agility, freedom of movement, and endurance to do the work for which he was developed.

Temperament—The Dachshund is clever, lively and courageous to the point of rashness, persevering in above and below-ground work, with all the senses well-developed. Any display of shyness is a serious fault.

Special Characteristics of the Three Coat Varieties—The Dachshund is bred with three varieties of coat: (1) smooth, (2) wirehaired, (3) longhaired, and is shown in two sizes, Standard and Miniature. All three varieties and both sizes must conform to the characteristics already specified. The following features are applicable for each variety.

Smooth Dachshund—Coat—Short, smooth and shining. Should be neither too long nor too thick. Ears not leathery.

Tail—Gradually tapered to a point, well but not too richly haired. Long sleek bristles on the underside are considered a patch of strong-growing hair, not a fault. A brush tail is a fault, as is also a partly or wholly hairless tail.

Color of Hair—Although base color is immaterial, certain patterns and basic colors predominate. One-colored Dachshunds include red (with or without a shading of interspersed dark hair or sable) and cream. A small amount of white on the chest is acceptable, but not desirable. Nose and nails—black.

Two-colored Dachshunds include black, chocolate, wild boar, gray (blue) and fawn (Isabella), each with tan markings over the eyes, on the sides of the jaw and underlip, on the inner edge of the ear, front, breast, inside and behind the front legs, on the paws and around the anus, and from there to about one-third to one-half of the length of the tail on the underside. Undue prominence or extreme lightness of tan markings is undesirable. A small amount of white on the chest is acceptable but not desirable. Nose and nails—in the case of black dogs, black; for chocolate and all other colors, dark brown, but self-colored is acceptable.

Dappled Dachshunds—The "single" dapple pattern is expressed as lighter-colored areas contrasting with the darker base color, which may be any acceptable color. Neither the light nor the dark color should predominate. Nose and nails are the same as for one and two-colored Dachshunds. Partial or wholly blue (wall) eyes are as acceptable as dark eyes. A large area of white on the chest of a dapple is permissible.

A "double" dapple is one in which varying amounts of white coloring occur over the body in addition to the dapple pattern. Nose and nails—as for one and two-colored Dachshunds; partial or wholly self-colored is permissible.

Brindle is a pattern (as opposed to a color) in which black or dark stripes occur over the entire body although in some specimens the pattern may be visible only in the tan points.

Wirehaired Dachshund—Coat—With the exception of jaw, eyebrows, and ears, the whole body is covered with a uniform tight, short, thick, rough, hard outer

A beautiful representative of the breed, and a truly great Dachshund.

coat but with finer, somewhat softer, shorter hairs (undercoat) everywhere distributed between the coarser hairs. The absence of an undercoat is a fault. The distinctive facial furnishings include a beard and eyebrows. On the ears the hair is shorter than on the body, almost smooth. The general arrangement of the hair is such that the wirehaired Dachshund, when viewed from a distance, resembles the smooth. Any sort of soft hair in the outercoat, wherever found on the body, especially on the top of the head, is a fault. The same is true of long, curly, or wavy hair, or hair that sticks out irregularly in all directions.

Tail—Robust, thickly haired, gradually tapering to a point. A flag tail is a fault.

Color of hair—While the most common colors are wild boar, black and tan, and various shades of red, all colors are admissible. A small amount of white on the chest, although acceptable, is not desirable.

Nose and nails—Same as for the smooth variety.

Longhaired Dachshund—Coat—The sleek, glistening, often slightly wavy hair is longer under the neck and on the forechest, the underside of the body, the ears, and behind the legs. The coat gives the dog an elegant appearance. Short hair on the ear is not desirable. Too profuse a coat which masks type, equally long hair all over the whole body, a curly coat, or a pronounced parting on the back are faults.

Tail—Carried gracefully in prolongation of the spine; the hair attains its greatest length here and forms a veritable flag.

Color of Hair—Same as for the smooth Dachshund.

Nose and nails—Same as for the smooth.

The foregoing description is that of the ideal Dachshund. Any deviation from the above described dog must be penalized to the extent of the deviation, keeping in mind the importance of the contribution of the various features toward the basic original purpose of the breed.

Disqualification—Knuckling over of front legs.

From top left: Judge Albert Van Court and Peggy Westphal showing Ch. Westphal's Shillalah in 1968.

chapter 7

Conformation and Appearance

Have ten people look at something blue, and there would be no disagreement among them as to what the color was. While shades may differ, blue is blue. The Standard for the Dachshund is not quite as simple as the nature and attributes of a color. The same ten people, when presented with a Dachshund, would have no question as to what breed the dog belonged to, but might completely disagree upon how it conforms to the Standard. This does not necessarily mean that they are all right or all wrong. People have subjective opinions, so in the same respect that it might occur that no two in the group of ten would entirely agree upon a favorite *shade* of blue, no two of the ten might agree upon a Dachshund's conformation to the Standard.

These differences of opinion are not limited to the Dachshund. They exist in every breed of dog. For lack of a better word, and to conform to the term generally accepted by breeders, I will refer to these gray areas as *type*. ("I?" you say. "I thought a 'we' was writing this book . . ." Well, being that I am an AKC judge, my co-author has agreed to leave this chapter to me!)

Each person has his own perception of the perfect Dachshund, and while the perfect dog has never been bred, breeders and judges alike should be drawn to three major considerations, namely type, balance, and function. Subsequently, each detail of conformation as interpreted from the Standard must be considered in proportion to the whole. No features should be exaggerated.

I prefer an elegant Dachshund. *Elegance* is defined in the dictionary as "having dignified richness and grace." Although an easy concept to conceive of, elegance is difficult to explain in words. Perhaps a good way to explain it may be to use a comparison between a pickup truck and a sports car. Each is a type of motor vehicle, and each has a definable form and function. Each part of a truck is strong and functional, but the pieces are often designed to perform independent of one another. The vehicle as a whole does not have the grace and smoothness of a sports car. One might assert that the pickup metaphorically represents the Dachshund's purpose as a hunting dog, while the sports car—with its speed, maneuverability, and subtleties—represents its purpose as a show dog. In short, I would choose a Jaguar over a pickup.

I will attempt, through words and drawings, to present our interpretation of the Standard. The type of Dog that I prefer begins with the premise that a Dachshund must be able to achieve, through conformation, what he is bred to do. Eye appeal is a byproduct of the perfectly blended pieces working in unison to achieve this objective.

Although I have successfully bred well over 100 Champions in all three varieties and both sizes, and as a multi-breed judge have examined show dogs numbering into the thousands since 1973, others have as well. In other words, the following is offered only as my opinion.

Before a Dachshund is placed on the table, where the primary examination is conducted, the entire class is moved around the ring so that the judge can get an overview of all the dogs present. When I see a smooth, free-moving dog going around my ring, I generally find that it will be well made, with all the correct proportions, once on the table.

The use of a table is not just because the dog is short and low to the ground, but it also helps the judges prevent leg and back pain. At waist level it is easier to feel how the dog is made. A Dachshund, being a scent hound, might be frightened by a judge coming down to meet him. Under no circumstances should a

The author examines the head and expression on the table.

judge ever try to touch a Dachshund other than on the table. (If after examination and being moved around the ring the judge should wish to reexamine the dog, the dog should be placed back on the table.)

When judging, if a dog is in motion and returning to me, I will always check temperament by putting my hand down in front of the dog to see whether he will come to me or shy away. Some jump up and think that I have a treat to offer them—this is acceptable and encouraged, as long as the dog sees you and is approaching you. Many good show dogs have been irreversibly frightened by a judge unexpectedly going down to meet them.

Once the handler has set up the dog, the judge has a maximum of two minutes to go over the animal and watch him move. There is much to look for, and several questions must be answered. The Dachshund is judged first from the side, and then from the front. The head is viewed and the oval chest felt. The topline, shoulders, and ribbing are examined from the side; the hocks and tail set from the rear.

One must remember that, according to the standard, the two sizes and three varieties of the Dachshund are the same and must be judged as such. Despite differences in the coat, conformation should not differ.

In considering type, judges must first ask themselves, "What was this animal bred for?" The answer for the Dachshund is to hunt small game and go to ground. The Dachshund must be long and low to the ground. The dog has to be made so that he can work all day in a field without tiring.

When I see a new Dachshund on the table I look for overall balance, and correct proportions. Following are the aspects of the dog that I consider:

- length of body relative to height
- if the head is in balance with the neck and body
- if it has a nice forechest
- if the front legs set properly under the chest
- if the ribbing is adequate to cover the heart and lungs
- if the topline is level, and the tail appears as a natural continuation of the backbone
- if the loin is short and strong, and the angle of the rear in balance with the front

The size of the Dachshund should not be a consideration at this time because the overall balance should be the same for both the Standard and the Miniature.

Now that the judge has an overall picture of the dog, the handler is asked to remove the dog from the table, and instructed to move the animal. Once in motion, the gait should be smooth and effortless. If made correctly, and all the body parts fit together in proper balance, the movement will be smooth.

I have stressed the importance of balance, form, and function from my perspective as a conformation judge. David Kawami, who has been very helpful with his knowledge of Field Trials and contributions to Chapter 11, "The Working Dachshund," presents the following practical essay on the reasons for, and the importance of, correct structure in the Dachshund:

For the past couple of years, I have been working on a video examining movement, particularly Dachshund movement. I have been encouraged by the late Constance Miller, author, AKC Judge, and Sight Hound breeder, and Rachel Page Elliot, author of *Dogsteps* (the book and video), and lecturer on dog movement. I can imagine that someone who has not seen a dog work a hole believes the Dachshund's short legs are solely designed to work earth. This is what I thought when I began videotaping Dachshunds and a Jack Russell Terrier moving through the earth. The illustrations of the Dachshund moving in a tunnel by Paul Brown in *The New Dachshund* by Lois Meistrell, and reprinted here, are interesting, and the best illustrations previously available. They are however, incorrect in my opinion, particularly the movement of the rear legs. What must be kept in mind is that the Dachshund does not work a tunnel for fun, he is working game. The game may be aggressive which means the Dachshund will be cautious, and give himself the option of backing out rapidly, or lunging forward to attack. The position of the rear legs in the Paul Brown illustration does not give the Dachshund the option of either. He is basically in the position of dragging his rear legs. The Dachshund pictured has limited forward movement, and no option to retreat. What the video shows is that the Dachshund keeps his weight over his legs (see illustration), not in front of his legs.

To understand this better, imagine you are standing and asked to lower yourself to half your height. This can be done in two ways: The first is to bend forward from the waist, a position that is awkward, and places you off balance. The second way is to flex at the knees, again awkward, but you retain your balance. The surprising thing the video shows is that a Jack Russel terrier with twice the length of leg of a Dachshund moves as easily through the tunnel as the Dachshund. Length of leg has little or no effect on the dog's ability to move through a tunnel. The limiting factor is depth of keel. This leaves the question of why does a Dachshund have short legs? The obvious answer is to move rapidly through the same type of terrain as the game he is pursuing; under and through brush instead of around or over it. The Dachshund is an all-around hunter, not just an earth dog. He is an excellent tracker who can be expected to work over a variety of rough terrain for hours.

Page Elliot points out that the most efficient gait is the trot, and while trotting around a flat ring of grass, or on rubber mats may demonstrate the dog is sound. The question is are you reluctant to work your dog in the field because he bruises and skins up his keel? If so, his legs may be too short, and his keel too deep. Constance Miller gave this advice on breeding 'just try to keep what you've got.' We do a disservice to the Dachshund if we strive for exaggeration; longer back, shorter legs, larger size, deeper keel.

David Kawami's rendition of a Dachshund moving through a tunnel.

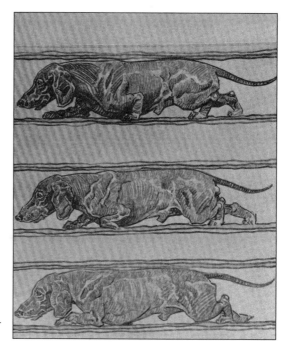

Dachshund working in an underground burrow.

Just as we do a disservice by breeding only for hunting abilities many of which are so complex genetically as to be ethereal. Keeping what you have is the real battle. Striving for an ideal is best left for inanimate objects that will not have to suffer our mistakes."

Now that you have a general idea of what must be considered by the judge, I will try to describe the correct Dachshund in more detail from my perspective—what I personally want to see in Dachshunds.

First and foremost, I want the Standard and Miniature to look alike. They must be viewed equally with no favoritism or bias. No special allowance

"Bred and shown in two sizes, Standard and Miniature, Miniatures are not a separate classification but compete in a class division for '11 pounds and under at 12 months of age and older.' Weight of the Standard size is usually between 16 and 32 pounds."–Quote from the Standard.

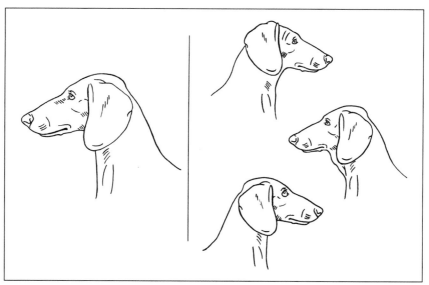

Illustration 1: The ideal head. The head should taper uniformly to the tip of the nose. The eyes are of medium size, almond-shaped with an energetic and pleasant expression. The skull should slope gradually with little perceptible stop into the finely-formed, slightly arched muzzle and the ears are set near the top of the head, not too far forward, and are of moderate length as pictured here. *Illustration 2:* This dog has ears that are set too high. *Illustration 3:* This dog has too much dewlap on throat. *Illustration 4:* This dog has eyes that are too large and round.

should be made for conformation flaws based solely on size. A Dachshund is a Dachshund. Period.

Viewed from the top and the side, the head should taper uniformly. The eyes are almond shaped with dark rims. A rim should be as dark as possible, preferably black, except in chocolate or light colored dogs. Round eyes detract from the soft gentle expression. The ears should frame the face and be set near the top of the skull in smooths and wires (they may be a little lower on the longhairs). Short ears take away from the expression. The skull should be slightly arched, neither broad nor narrow, and slightly sloped with very little stop. The muzzle should be in balance with the back of the skull and should also be slightly arched. The nose should be black and well open. The lips should be stretched tightly and cover the lower jaw. The lower jaw must be full. I view a weak underjaw as a serious flaw—and it is a problem with the breed which appears to be increasing. One must remember that the Dachshund is a hunter and needs a strong lower jaw to grasp and hold his prey. The teeth should form a scissors bite, but one which is at least level is not a very serious a problem for me.

The forequarters of the Dachshund are perhaps the most important factor for me. The perfect *front* is perhaps the least understood and most difficult element to find in the Dachshund (as well as in many other breeds)

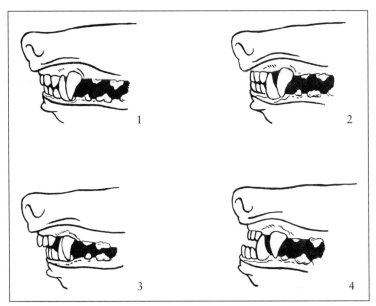

Illustration 1: Correct scissors bite. "Powerful canine teeth; teeth fit closely together in a scissors bite."–Quote from the Standard. *Illustration 2:* "An even bite is a minor fault."–Quote from the Standard. This is also known as a level or pincer bite. *Illustration 3:* This bite is overshot, the lower jaw recedes. This is a serious fault. *Illustration 4:* This bite is undershot, the under jaw is longer than the upper one. This is also a serious fault.

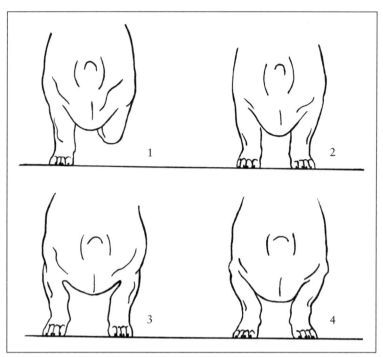

Illustration 1: "Viewed from the front, the legs do not move in exact parallel plane, but incline slightly inward to compensate for shortness of leg and width of chest." –Quote from the Standard. *Illustration 2:* "When viewed from the front, the thorax appears oval and extends downward to the midpoint of the forearm."–Quote from the Standard. *Illustration 3:* The front is incorrect. The chest is round and wide, the legs are too far apart. *Illustration 4:* This front is also incorrect. Often called a "fiddle front" the elbows are wide apart, forearms slope inward and feet are turned out.

conformation. One must constantly remind himself that the Dachshund must be able to dig, go to ground, and have the stamina to do a day's work. The dog must have an oval chest to fit properly with the correct shoulder assembly, and should extend to the midpoint of the arm. The shoulder blades are long, and ideally the upper arm is the same length as the lower. Short upper arms cause the dog to paddle and not move smoothly, making digging, going to ground, and freedom of movement more difficult. Correct shoulder blades and upper arms, though difficult to find, are a huge plus for me as a judge, whereas a "straight" front, lacking in angle, is a negative even if the rest of the dog's conformation is excellent.

The forearm should wrap around the oval chest with minimum protrusion of the elbow. The feet, also very important, should be tight and full with thick pads and well-arched toes. Besides a flat-footed Dachshund not being able to dig very long or work in the field, they are not pleasing to the eye. For this reason, keeping a dog's nails short is a must.

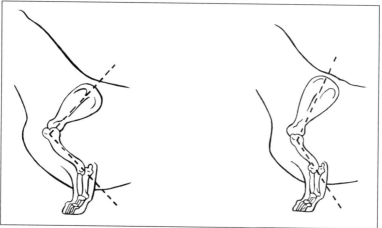

Illustration 1: "Upper Arm—Ideally the same length as the shoulder blade and at right angles to the latter . . ."–Quote from the Standard. *Illustration 2:* This front is incorrect, the shoulder blade and the upper arm join at an angle greater than 90 degrees, and the upper arm is too short.

The trunk of the Dachshund should be long and well-muscled and as straight as possible between the withers and the short loin. The ribs should be well sprung, and the keel of sufficient length to cover the heart and lungs. The underline has a slight tuck up.

The hindquarters must be strong and muscled. The pelvis, thigh, and second thigh are ideally the same length and form a series of right angles. Viewed from the rear, neither should turn in or out. The hind paws are smaller than the front, but should still have thick pads and well-arched toes. The tail is a continuation of the spine and should not be carried over the back. It may be carried outward or slope down, but never between the legs.

The Dachshund's gait should be smooth and effortless. From the side, the dog should have good reach in front and good extending drive in the rear. When coming at you, the front will incline slightly inward because of the short legs. When going away, you should be able to see the rear pads.

As previously mentioned, the temperament of the Dachshund is of prime importance. Shyness of any kind is unacceptable and should not be tolerated by the judge. The Standard calls for the Dachshund to be clever, lively, and courageous to the point of rashness.

To the best of everyone in the dog world's knowledge, the perfect dog has not yet been bred. Perfection is what reputable breeders constantly strive for in every litter they breed. As a judge I have seen many excellent specimens of the breed, but never one that could not be faulted in some manner. Since perfection is, at least so far, not a reality, the key is to look for overall balance and type.

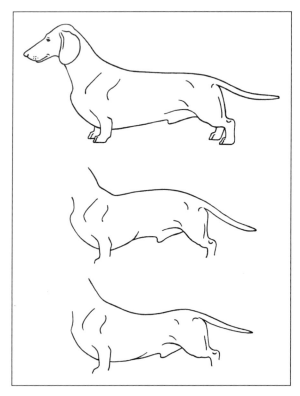

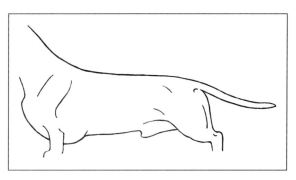

"The keel merges gradually into the line of the abdomen and extends well beyond the front legs."–Quote from the Standard.

This is an example of ribbing that is too short and stops too abruptly.

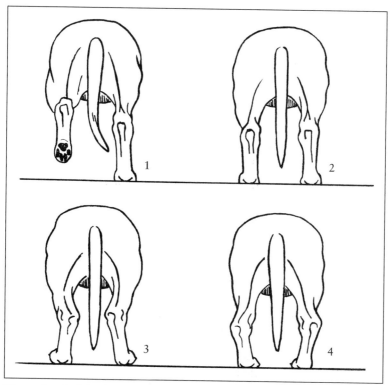

Illustration 1: "The thrust of correct movement is seen when the rear pads are clearly exposed during rear extension. Feet must travel parallel to the line of motion with no tendency to swing out, cross over, or interfere with each other."–Quote from the Standard. *Illustration 2:* "From the rear, the thighs are strong and powerful. The legs turn neither in nor out."–Quote from the Standard. *Illustration 3:* This rear is incorrect because the hocks turn inward. This is known as "cow hocks". *Illustration 4:* This rear is incorrect. The hocks turn outward and toes turn in.

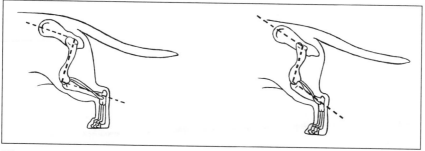

Illustration 1: "The pelvis, the thigh, the second thigh, and the metatarsus are ideally the same length . . ."–Quote from the Standard. A series of right angles should form as the pelvis, the thigh and the second thigh join as shown. *Illustration 2:* This rear is not correct, the hindquarters are too narrow. The pelvis, the thigh and the second thigh do not form a series of right angles because they join at angles which are incorrect and are not all the same length.

Illustration 1: "Gait—fluid and smooth. Forelegs reach well forward, without much lift, in unison with the driving action of hind legs." –Quote from the Standard. *Illustration 2:* This dog's movement is incorrect. His gait is shorter-stepping due to poor angulation in front and rear.

The Author, presenting a conformation ribbon to Gina Leone. Note the correct front shoulders.

chapter 8

Color

Most people think that Dachshunds come in only two colors (red, and black and tan). Those of us in the Dachshund fancy know better, having had a wider range of experience with the breed and access to the many reference materials available on it.

A large selection of colors and patterns are available in the Dachshund. Understanding the difference between color and pattern is a necessarily basic concept. Color is the base on which the pattern is set. Color in Dachshunds is red (two different kinds), black and tan, chocolate and tan, isabella and tan, and sable/wild boar.

Patterns affect the expression of color. The patterns present in the Dachshund are as follows: self (solid color), dappling (merling), brindling (stripes), and piebald (white spotting). Theoretically, any pattern can occur on any color.

GENES

Genes are the little determiners of everything a dog is or is going to be. Genes are part of his chromosomes, are present in every cell in his body, and hold all of the information needed to make the dog whatever color he will be. Each color gene determines one specific characteristic. In the domestic dog, there are ten gene series identified that affect color and pattern: A, B, C, D, E, G, M, S, R, and T, with the possibility of another color gene series, P (Little, 1973).

Each gene series has several different versions of that gene present, called *alleles*. Not all of the alleles of each gene series in the domestic dog are present in the Dachshund, but the ones that affect color in the Dachshund are listed below (the dominant allele first, the most recessive last):

A: ay (red, tan); aw (sable/wild boar); at (tan points)

B: B (black); b (chocolate)

C: C (full pigmentation); cch (reduced pigment, or chinchilla dilution)

D: D (intense pigmentation); d (blue dilution)

E: ebr (brindle); E (solid coat color); e (restriction, or the recessive red)

G: g (no progressive graying over a lifetime)

M: M (dappling); m (solid color)

S: S (self, or completely pigmented body surface); Sp (piebald white spotting)

T: T (ticking); t (no ticking)

Since Dr. Clarence C. Little provides an in-depth discussion of each gene and its alleles in his book, *The Inheritance of Coat Color in Dogs,* discussing each gene here would be cumbersome; only those relevant to the color or pattern being discussed will be presented here in writing out the genetic formula for that color or pattern. For example, a red dog could be ayayBBCCDDEEggmmSStt in total formula, but in the discussion of that particular red dog, only the *ayay* or *ayayBB* part would be relevant. All animals possess only two alleles of each gene series—no more, no less.

The terms *dominant* and *recessive* need to be explained. Little defines them as follows: "In an ordinary pair [of genes] . . . the one of the pair which masks or conceals the other is called dominant, and the one which is masked, or concealed, recessive" (p. 16). For example, dappling (M) is dominant to solid (m); a pair of genes present in a dog as Mm will make it a dapple, even though it carries one gene for solid color.

Two more important terms are *homozygous* and *heterozygous*. A dog which is a homozygous red, *ayay* in genetic formula, can produce nothing but reds. A heterozygous red on the other hand is usually *ayat* and can produce the tan-point colors as well (i.e., black and tan, chocolate and tan, etc.).

Finally, the difference between *phenotype* and *genotype* must be understood. Phenotype is the actual physical appearance of the dog, the expression of the color genes you actually see. Genotype is the dog's genetic makeup and also includes the recessive, or hidden, genes which do not manifest themselves in the dog's physical appearance.

Color Inheritance

RED

There are two different types of red in the Dachshund. The first is the one with which most of us are already familiar, the dominant red, which is due to the action of the *ay* allele. A homozygous red is *ayay*, and is incapable of producing any color other than red. The phenotypic appearance of both kinds of heterozygous reds is the same as that of the homozygous red; (1) *ayat*, which can produce the tan-pointed colors in addition to red, and (2) *ayaw*, which can produce the sable/wild boar color as well as red.

Most red Dachshunds carry at least one B allele; they can be BB (homozygous) or Bb (heterozygous carrying a recessive for chocolate).

When the red dog has no B gene, his nose and nails will be brown, even though his body coloration is red because both genes he possesses in the B series would be bb. It is possible for a brown-nosed red to produce chocolate and tan, but only if that brown-nosed red is heterozygous in the A series *ayat*. If this brown-nosed red were homozygous red, he would be incapable of producing chocolate and tan.

The second type of red present in the Dachshund is in a different gene series (E) from the first (A series red), and unlike A reds, this red is recessive. Recessive red is expressed when ee appears on a dog that is not ayay but atat. The recessive red's genetic formula would be atatee. This kind of red can appear from two black and tan parents, and there will not be a single dark hair anywhere on the body.

BLACK AND TAN

Black and tan is produced when the genes combine as *atatBB* or *atatBb* (the latter carrying chocolate). A black and tan can be produced by two red parents as long as both are *ayat*. Curiously, a black and tan can be produced if one parent is a blue and tan (atatBBdd) and the other parent is chocolate and tan (atatbbDD); the resulting puppy's formula would then be *atatBbDd*, which allows him to be black and tan (capable of producing isabella and tan).

CHOCOLATE AND TAN

Chocolate and tan occurs when the dog's formula is *atatbb*. For example, chocolate and tan may be produced by two black and tans that carry the chocolate gene (atatBb), by two reds carrying both the chocolate (b) and the tan-points (at) gene, or by the brown-nosed red described above. As long as each parent has one tan-points gene and one chocolate gene, they can produce chocolate and tan offspring.

When discussing chocolate and tan, it is important to remember the difference between a brown-nosed red and a true chocolate and tan. A dog that has a brown nose and brown nails is not necessarily a chocolate and tan; in order to be a chocolate and tan, the dog must have visible, easily distinguished tan points akin to those present on a black and tan. No matter how light-colored the chocolate part of the coat is, it will always be a different color from the tan points. If no tan points such as those on a black and tan can be found, then the dog is not chocolate and tan.

BLUE DILUTION

The blue dilution factor (d) is needed to produce blue and tan (steel blue or bluish-gray, with pale tan points) or isabella and tan (silvery gray color like that of a Weimaraner, with pale tan points). In order to have the dilution gene affect the dog it must be present as *dd*, as the D form of the gene is dominant to d. Blue and tans are actually diluted black and tans, *atatBBdd,* or *atatBbdd* (carrying a chocolate recessive). The gene for dilution, d, must be carried by both parents in order to produce a diluted pup. Dilution does not just affect the black and tan; the dilute gene d can produce isabella and tan (*atatbbdd*—diluted chocolate and tan). Blues and isabellas occasionally have thin hair coats and/or bald patches and skin problems; such animals or any of their offspring should not be used for breeding.

Dilution in the D series can also affect reds, producing a "washed-out" or yellow-red appearance; such a dog would have a blue nose and blue nails.

CHINCHILLA DILUTION

There is a second type of dilution believed to be present in the Dachshund, that in the C series as *Cch*, also known as the "chinchilla" gene. The gene C (full pigmentation) is incompletely dominant over the chinchilla gene (reduced pigmentation). For example, a red dog that is *CC* should be intensely red, darker than the dog that is *CCch*, and in turn, *CCch* will be darker than a dog that is *CchCch*. In the Dachshund, there is a wealth of evidence that the chinchilla gene is spread among the population. Although incapable of affecting black pigment, the chinchilla gene can work on any tan or red coloration and is probably responsible for some of the wide range in depth of color in reds and in the tan points on black and tan dogs. Also, while unable to affect black pigment, it can act on chocolate; witness the wide range of

The first two blue dapple Champions, Ch. Taramanor's Ethereal Blue (left) and Ch. Gingerbreds Don Juan (right).

colors in Chesapeake Bay Retrievers, which Little documented as being caused by the chinchilla gene. All Chesapeakes are *bb* (chocolate), which allows the chinchilla gene to act; the darkest are probably *bbCC*, the intermediate ones *bbCCch*, and the lightest, straw-colored are *bbcchcch*. In Dachshunds, it is possible that those black and tans with yellow-tan points are *CCch*, or even possibly *CchCch*.

The chinchilla gene is most likely responsible for the recently apparent creams in Miniature longs, and for the very light wheaten wires (*ayaycchcch* or *ayatcchcch*, dominant red paled to cream by chinchilla, or *atatcchcchee*, recessive red paled to cream by chinchilla).

SABLE/WILD BOAR

The term "sable" is commonly misused to describe a longhair with a heavy black overlay or an interspersion of black hairs on the back and neck. A dog that fits this description is not a true sable; sable in Dachshunds is a distinct, inheritable color by itself.

A true sable longhair (*awaw* or *awat*) will appear from a distance to be black and tan. Marked like a black and tan, the undercoat beneath the "black" part of his coat is red. There is a possibility for the tan on the face to extend to a red mask instead of just "normal" tan markings. True sable longhairs are currently very rare.

Wild boar smooths and wires are caused by the same *aw* gene as sable in longhairs, the only difference being the terminology used with respect to the coat. Since the hair is shorter on wires (and of course on smooths) than on longhairs, the wild boar wire or smooth appears to have more red than sable longhairs. This is simply because the undercoat is easier to see when the outer coat or guard hairs are short. The extent of the markings is the same in wild boar smooths and wires as it is in sable longhairs.

Breeders should avoid registering any puppy as sable or wild boar before it reaches full maturity, as many reds may start out as visual sable/wild boar, but are clearly not by the time they are six or seven months old.

Pattern Inheritance

There are four patterns present in Dachshunds: self (solid color), dapple (merle), brindle (stripes), and piebald (white spotting). Dapple and brindle are dominant to solid color; piebald white spotting is recessive to solid color. Each pattern is not a color itself, but is a factor affecting color.

SELF

The self pattern is shown in any dog that does not express dappling, brindling, or piebald white spotting. All the basic colors described above under color inheritance are self colors.

DAPPLE

Dappling is represented by the M gene. The non-dappled dog is *mm*. The heterozygous, or "single" dapple (the kind with which most of us are familiar), is *Mm*. The heterozygous dapple has lighter patches of whatever ground (self) color he is, randomly spaced on his body in a ragged fashion. On a black and tan, dappling is expressed as splashes of gray or silver. The red dapple has lighter patches of red; the chocolate dapple, cream-colored patches; blue dapple, lighter bluish-gray patches. In the tan-pointed colors, the dapple gene does not seem to be able to affect the tan points if the dog is a heterozygous dapple. Bred to a solid-color (self) dog, a heterozygous dapple will produce more heterozygous dapples at an average ratio of fifty percent dapple and fifty percent solid-colored puppies.

The homozygous, or "double," dapple is *MM* in formula, and can be obtained by breeding two heterozygous dapples; the double dapple will show up on average as one out of four in such a breeding. The double dapple will have varying amounts of white on his body. The amount of white present will range from four white feet, a white-tipped tail, and one or two small white spots elsewhere on the body to the extreme case of the nearly-all white dog with perhaps only a few random colored spots which indicate the base color.

The dapple gene in the homozygous state is termed semi-lethal, because it can have various deleterious effects. A double dapple puppy may die in the uterus or be stillborn. He may be blind, deaf, or both; or, when he opens his eyelids, may have very small eyes or even lack eyes all together. In the heavily white-marked double, at least one and possibly both eyes will be blue. The double dapple is completely incapable of producing anything but dapple pups. The blindness and/or deafness of the double dapple is not an inherited type in that it will not be passed on to any heterozygous dapple offspring. Blindness and deafness in the dapple Dachshund is only a possibility in the homozygous condition.

The single advantage of having a dog that is only capable of producing dapple puppies is far outweighed by the disabilities with which the dog is

Ch. Brandachs Blue Zircon, the first double blue and tan dapple Miniature longhair Champion in the U.S. and Canada.

burdened when born a homozygous dapple. More than likely he will be either blind or deaf, or have limited eyesight and/or hearing. This will severely affect his ability to function as a normal pet. Of the double dapples I have encountered, none have lived a normal Dachshund lifespan of fourteen or more years—their lives possibly shortened by the lethal effects of being *MM*. Deliberately creating a double dapple is, in most cases, unethical and should be discouraged.

Double dapple longhair as seen on both the left and right sides.

Double black and tan Standard longhair dapple. Note reduced eye size.

Sangsavant D'Appalussa, Standard longhair double black and tan dapple. "Dap" was never shown because he was deaf; however, he is the sire of several show Champions.

BRINDLE

Brindling is a pattern present in the E series as *ebr* and expressed as dark stripes all over the dog's body, running from the midline down to the belly. The *ebr* allele is dominant to E (solid color) and e (recessive red). A red brindle would usually be *ayayebrE* (homozygous red, heterozygous brindle), *ayatebrE* (heterozygous red carrying tan points, heterozygous brindle), or either of the two preceding formulas but with *ebrebr* instead of *ebre*. The brindle that is *ayayebrE* could produce a black and tan brindle if bred to another dog with the same formula. Brindling affects all parts of the hair coat, but since a black and tan is already mostly black, the stripes show up only in the tan points. If a brindle happened to carry no genes for black (if it were, for example, *bb* instead of *BB* or *Bb*) then the stripes would be chocolate-colored and the nose and nails would be brown. If a brindle carried two genes for blue dilution (dd), then the stripes, nose, and nails would be blue. The intensity of the brindling on a red varies from dog to dog, and may range from the nearly clear red with a few very distinct stripes to the dog that is so heavily brindled that it appears nearly black (with no tan points).

Mother and daughter are both red brindles, demonstrating the wide range in the intensity of striping possible with the brindle pattern.

PIEBALD WHITE SPOTTING

Piebald white spotting was first documented in Dachshunds by Dr. C. William Nixon in Lois Meistrell's book, *The New Dachshund*. Unlike dappling, piebald white spotting is recessive, the *Sp* gene in the S series; the dominant member is S (solid color). A piebald white spotted dog would be *SpSp*. It can occur in connection with any color as well as any other pattern. The white smooth Miniature Dachshund, seen in Australia in the 1980s, may possibly have been marked by the extreme-white gene in the S series, *Sw* in the homozygous condition (immediately after she appeared, the Australian Standard was revised to disallow an all-white Dachshund). The genes in the S series are also incompletely dominant (listed from most dominant to most recessive): *S, Si* (Irish spotting, as seen in the Basenji), *Sp, Sw*.

In breeding piebald white-spotted Dachshunds, Dr. C. William Nixon also found another gene at work—the T gene for "ticking." In his article, "The Incorporation of Two New Patterning Factors into the Coat Color Complement of Dachshunds" in *The American Dachshund*, he noted that ticking had occurred on the piebalds that he had bred and believed that this gene was introduced at the same time as piebald white spotting.

COLOR PIONEERS

Much credit must go to the first breeders who involved themselves with the "other color" Dachshunds. Few, but determined and dedicated, they have left us a legacy of quality dapples, chocolates, brindles, etc., that we are privileged to be able to work with. Certainly the first who deserves mention is Mrs. Justine Cellarius, who bred the first dapple Dachshund Champion, Ch. Uhlan v Cellarius (Standard smooth, finished 1942). It was not until the late 1960's, some twenty-five years or so after Uhlan, that another dapple

Ch. Cinnabar Candy Man, the first dapple Dachshund to win Best in Show in America, and the first long-haired dapple to win a group. Owned by Barbara Keck and Alice Dildine; handled by Howard Nygood.

finished, Ch. Wagatomo Tessella L (Standard long). Tessela, bred by Dr. Miles K. McElrath and owned by Grover and Beverly Schlitz, was the first Champion dapple Dachshund bitch. She was also the first longhair dapple Champion and the first Champion chocolate dapple. Dr. McElrath paved much of the road leading to the production of quality "other color" Standard longhairs and smooths; his original dapple stock came from Mary F. Dean, who frequented the California show scene in the 1960's with smooth dapples and blues of such quality that in a more color-tolerant show atmosphere they could have easily finished their titles.

There was a 28-year gap between Ch. Uhlan v Cellarius and the next Standard smooth dapple Champion, Ch. Karlstadt's Mahareshi, finished in 1970 by the late Barbara Murphy. At the same time, more Standard long dapples from Dr. McElrath's Wagatomo Kennels were finishing their titles as well, and Patricia Crary purchased dapple Wagatomo stock and added to the dapple accomplishments with Champion Standard smooths and longhairs.

In 1975 a breeding between Patricia Crary's Sangsavant D'Appalussa (Standard longhair double black and tan dapple) and Sharon Cox's Gingerblue Rose of Sharon (blue and tan Standard smooth) set the stage for producing the first blue dapple Champion, Ch. Gingerbreds Don Juan, and the second blue dapple Champion, Ch. Taramanor's Ethereal Blue. Ethereal Blue sired the first double dapple Standard Champion, Ch. Serendipity's Double Trouble (double blue and tan dapple), finished in 1986, bred by Ann Irwin and Charles Johnson and owned by Bill and Susan Madden.

Longtime Dachshund breeders and judges Philip and Eleanor Bishop bred the first blue and tan Champion, Ch. Lynsulee V Copano Bluebelle (Standard smooth, that was later sold to the late Maria Hayes). In the late 1970's the first chocolate and tan Standard long finished, Ch. Randolph's Charles

Ch. Serendipity's Double Trouble, the first double blue dapple Champion.

Le Brun, bred and owned by Norah Randolph. Dorothy and Diane Poranski have been actively breeding quality chocolate smooth Standards for over thirty years. Diane believes the first chocolate and tan Standard smooth Champion was owned by the late John Cook.

In 1971, Miniatures struck pay dirt with the first dapple Miniature Champion, a wirehair, Ch. Calpreta Print of Cumtru. "Printa" was imported from England and owned by the late Stanley and Carol Orne. The third smooth dapple Champion and the first Miniature smooth dapple Champion was Ch. Midachs Penthouse Joker M (black and tan dapple), bred by Sharon Michael and owned by Howard Atlee, finished in 1974.

Also in 1974, the first dapple Miniature longhair Champion finished, Ch. Barbemac's Fancy Colours ML, Bred by Irene Casto and owned by Mary Sue Humphries and Virginia MacLeod. "Bina" produced from her first litter the first dapple Miniature longhair in Canada, Can. Ch. Barbemac's Diamond Girl ML, owned by Irene Swartman. Diamond Girl produced the first dapple Miniature longhair male Champion in Canada, Can. Ch. Melrene's Demi Silver Nugget, bred and owned by Irene Swartman. Shortly after Bina finished, the first dapple Miniature longhair male Champion also finished, Ch. Dachsheider's Silver Diamond, bred and owned by Irene Castro. Diamond left us a large legacy of quality Miniature longhair dapples, many of which were bred by Mrs. Castro, who for over 40 years has been breeding Miniatures in all three coats and a multitude of colors.

The first chocolate dapple Miniature longhair Champion, Ch. Wildwood Sea Shadow ML, bred by Martha and John Fuller and owned by Ann Schoolcraft, finished in 1983. The second chocolate and tan dapple Miniature longhair Champion (and the first bitch) was Ch. Wildwood Tropical Trend ML, finished in 1986, also bred by Martha and John Fuller and owned by Debbie Hanselka.

Ch. Barbemac's Fancy Colours, the first dapple Miniature longhair Champion in the U.S.

Ch. Dachsheider's Silver Diamond, the first male dapple Miniature longhair Champion.

Another landmark was achieved in 1980, when Ch. Wilhelm's Snow Night (Miniature smooth), owned by Joy Perry and William S. Chappell, became the first double dapple Miniature Champion.

In 1993, history was made at the Dachshund Club of America's national specialty where Gwen Wexler won Winners Bitch with her double black and tan dapple Miniature longhair bitch, Westerly White Roses. This win finished "Sheltie" (and nearly Gwen!). It was the first time a double dapple had won at the national specialty, and Sheltie became the second double dapple Miniature Champion and the first double dapple longhair Miniature Champion. Following in Sheltie's footsteps in very short order was Am/Can. Ch. Brandach's Blue Zircon. Bred and owned by Patricia Taylor, she became the first double dapple Miniature to be titled in the United States and Canada, the first double blue and tan dapple Miniature Champion, and the first double dapple to win at the National Miniature Dachshund Club's specialty show, the NMDC Expo, in September 1993, where she was Winners Bitch and Best of Winners. Her sire, Am/Can Ch. Auslagen Silver Smythe MLDD was the first double dapple Miniature male Champion (any coat), bred and owned by Jeanie Kolstad.

At present, there are no double dapple wire Champions of either size.

In 1974, show breeders rediscovered the brindle gene in the breed, and most, if not all, of the brindle Dachshunds present in the United States today come from lines leading back to one black and tan brindle Standard long bitch owned by Carol Piper, Shannopin's Sweet Dream L. "Dagmar" was bred twice to Ch. Kemper Dachs Bjorn (Best of Breed, DCA '74), producing one red brindle bitch in each litter. From the first litter, Chatham's Tiger Ballad went to the late Maria Hayes, and from the second litter Chatham's Tiger Cantata went to Mary Sue Humphries.

Four generations away from Ballad, the first brindle Miniature Champion finished in 1983, Ch. Dachsheider's Gambler ML, bred and owned by

Ch. Dachsheider's Gambler, the first brindle Miniature Champion.

Irene Casto. Gambler sired Mary Sue Humphries' first brindle Champion, Ch. Barbemac's Tiger Amaryllis L (black and tan brindle, finished 1986), out of a daughter of Cantata. Gambler was also the first brindle Champion to finish in 43 years, since Ch. Hanne-Lore VD Waldhuette (finished 1940, a black and tan brindle). Gambler's litter sister, Ch. Dachsheider's Gidget II, also bred and owned by Irene Casto, became the first brindle Miniature Champion bitch when she finished in 1984. Unfortunately, the Standard longhair brindle males from the Bjorn/Dagmar breedings were not used, and at present Ch. Hanne-Lore remains the only Standard brindle Champion. There are also no smooth or wire brindle Champions of either size as of this writing.

Miniature breeder Helen Hollingsworth broke ground with a color which was virtually unknown in the United States before 1990 by showing and finishing her cream Miniature longhair, Ch. Priorsgate Peter Piper, imported from England. Since "Champers" finished, Helen has brought over quite a few more cream Mini longs and now boasts several cream Miniature longhair Champions.

Another Miniature breeder, Derryll Packer accomplished several firsts for the "colored" Dachshund in 1991 and 1992 by finishing Ch. Packer's My Li'l Freckles MS (first chocolate dapple smooth Mini Champion), Ch. Packer's Li'l Twix ML (first chocolate and tan Mini long bitch Champion), and Ch. Packer's Mocha Delite MS (first chocolate and tan Mini smooth Champion). Included in four generations of winning chocolate Miniature longhairs are Twix's and Freckles' sire, Ch. Jo An Jo's Packer's O Henry ML (the third chocolate and tan Miniature longhair Champion). Ch. DDD's Chocolate Chassis ML, bred and owned by Sandra Dickens (first chocolate and tan Miniature longhair Champion), sired Ch. Jo An Jo's Chocolate Express ML, bred and owned by Joan Oates (second chocolate and tan Miniature longhair Champion), who in turn sired Ch. Jo An Jo's Packer's O Henry ML, bred by Joan Oates, and owned by Derryll Packer, and the fourth generation is Twix's and Freckles' half-sister (same sire), Ch. Barbemac Parfait Chocolate ML (chocolate dapple bitch, finished 1994, granddaughter of the

Ch. Priorsgate Peter Piper, the first cream Champion in the U.S.

Ch. Shemby's MWNT Gold, the first female cream Champion in the U.S.

first chocolate dapple Mini long Champion), bred and owned by Mary Sue Humphries and the first chocolate dapple to capture a major award at the parent specialty (Best of Opposite to Best of Variety, DCA '95).

The first piebald Dachshund Champion finished in October 1995, Ch. Duchwood's Cornerstone MS, bred by Sandra and Douglas Russel and owned by Sandra. The first Miniature wirehair piebald Champion finished in April 1996, Ch. Domino's Lil Pumpkin Patch MW, bred and owned by Melissa Keshlaer.

Many Dachshund breeders have been involved in producing quality "other color" Dachshunds over the past forty years, and if we have left anyone out who should have been mentioned, it was most certainly not intentional. All of them deserve credit for helping to establish the quality "other color" Dachshunds, which were for so long denied the same considerations in the show ring as reds, and black and tans, and for demonstrating to judges and the show world in general that "other color" Dachshunds can hold their own in type and quality beneath the overlying fancier trappings.

Ch. Barbemac Parfait
Chocolat, chocolate dapple.

Ch. Duchwood's Corner-
stone MS, first piebald
Champion.

Ethical Considerations

Breeding of the "colored" Dachshund should never take precedence over breeding for correct conformation and temperament. A dog that is an unusual color,
or has a "perfect" pattern is useless if the underlying conformation or temperament does not warrant using that animal for breeding. Future generations of
quality Dachshunds depend on every breeder embracing the motto, "Quality
First, Color Second." There is nothing to be gained in producing a colored dog
with poor conformation or poor temperament, and that applies as much to
"normal" reds and black and tans as it does to dapples, brindles, chocolates,
and blues. There are more than enough dogs in the world that need good homes.
Breeding a litter merely to see what colors can be created with no regard for
improving the breed as a whole is irresponsible, and in some cases even cruel.

In the early 1950s Ch. Hardway Welcome Stranger established a breed record when he finished his championship by winning Best in Show from the classes at the Old Dominion Kennel Club and then within the next month was Best in Show three more times at major Eastern events. He topped the 1953 Specialty and was Best of Breed at one of the last of the great Morris and Essex Kennel Club shows. Bred, owned, and handled by Jeannette W. Cross.

References

Little, Clarence C. Sc.D. *The Inheritance of Coat Color in Dogs.* Howell Book House, New York, 1973.

McElrath, Dr. Miles K. "From 'Rags' to Dapple Dachshunds—A Summary History of Wagatomo Kennels." *The American Dachshund,* 35(1); A41-A56; Sept. 1973.

Meistrell, Lois. *The New Dachshund.* Howell Book House, New York, 1976.

Nixon, C. William. "The Incorporation of Two New Patterning Factors into the Coat Color Complement of Dachshunds." *The American Dachshund,* 40(3) 5-7; Jan./Feb. 1979.

chapter 9

Conformation Showing and Breeding

If you're thinking of showing your dog, it's probably for one of two reasons. You either think your dog is the most beautiful Dachshund you have ever seen and would like to know if she is as perfect as you think, or you bought her after careful study and advice from breeders with the intent of showing her.

If you want to breed her, it may be because you desire to fulfill her motherly instincts or just want to make some money. Or perhaps you wish to better the breed and produce puppies of show quality.

If your motivation arises from the first reason in either instance, we will try to dissuade you and give you our reasons. If you are serious about showing and breeding now and in the future, we hope our guidance will be helpful.

An AKC sanctioned dog show is not a beauty pageant. It's a well-organized, well-orchestrated forum for devoted breeders to display their dogs in a highly competitive environment. Often paid professional handlers are used. The judges may be either amateurs or professional, but all have been approved by the AKC. Many are licensed to judge only one breed. Some (relatively few) are "all arounders," qualified to judge all breeds. Most are either former professional handlers, or active or former breeders. Affectionately known as a "poochie parade," a dog show is serious business, not an arena for your pet.

From reading the chapters on the Dachshund Standard and conformation, you might conceivably have the impression that your Dachshund is made up of several definable pieces, the whole being the sum of its parts. On the contrary, a judge begins with the whole and then analyzes the pieces. Your

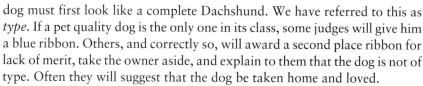

dog must first look like a complete Dachshund. We have referred to this as *type*. If a pet quality dog is the only one in its class, some judges will give him a blue ribbon. Others, and correctly so, will award a second place ribbon for lack of merit, take the owner aside, and explain to them that the dog is not of type. Often they will suggest that the dog be taken home and loved.

Judges' decisions are based on two main factors. Each dog is judged against the Standard for the breed without regard to the other dogs in the ring. Each dog is also judged against the others. The judge tries to pick those dogs nearest to the ideal type and appear to be physically and mentally sound. Rules require that each dog be individually examined. Teeth, eyes, coat, and structure are checked.

Males must have both testicles descended into the scrotum (neutered males and spayed females are not eligible for competition). Dogs are asked to move and are checked from the front, rear, and side for soundness. Limping or lameness requires that the dog be excused from further judging. Any dog attempting to bite a judge will also be excused.

Certain breeds may be measured for size. This does not apply to Dachshunds, but if a Dachshund is entered in the Miniature classes, he is subject to being weighed, and if found to be overweight (if he exceeds eleven pounds) and is at least one year of age, he will be excused.

Before entering your dog, we suggest attending a show as an observer. Watch the judge's instructions and the way the handlers present their dogs. Don't be afraid to talk with people and ask questions. Above all, observe, listen, and enjoy. The primary purpose of a dog show is to enable owners to exhibit their dogs in competition with others of his kind. The ultimate objective is to improve the quality of all purebred dogs through an intelligent breeding program using the dogs which have been proven to be, through such competition, the better representatives of their breeds.

The author presenting a first place ribbon to Ch. B's Javelin De Bayard, shown by breeder-owner Hannelore Heller. A beautiful representative of the breed and the foundation for many of today's pedigrees.

For the novice, shows can be very confusing. Following is a concise explanation of what to expect—from the basics through Best in Show.

There are two types of shows—specialties, which are restricted to one breed, and all-breed shows open to all AKC-recognized breeds (which today number over 130 and the list is still growing).

There are three organizations which govern dog shows. The first is a sponsoring kennel club, which is a member of the AKC. It selects a date and location for the show, which must then be approved by the AKC. It is responsible for obtaining the show grounds, selecting judges, providing maintenance, food, sanitation, security, general operation, and prizes.

Next is the superintendent, one of several companies whose sole purpose is to put on the show. Prior to the show date, it prints and mails a premium list to prospective entrants. The list includes the date and location of the show, the names of the judges and the breeds that they will judge, a request for an entry fee (currently between $16 and $20 per dog), and entry forms which may be mailed or faxed back to the superintendent. Lists are distributed six weeks in advance of the show date, and entries close three weeks prior to the show. You may either mail or fax your entries, and five days prior to the show you will receive an entry form which must be presented at the gate entitling both you and your dog entry onto the show grounds.

Approximately one week prior to the show, the superintendent will mail a judging schedule to each entrant. This gives the time of the show, ring numbers where their dogs will be judged, and the numbers and sexes of the dogs entered in each breed. The day before the show, the superintendent will provide and set-up tenting (if outdoors) and all required rings. On the day of the show, they collect signed sheets from the judges indicating the placement of the dogs and forward these to the AKC where records are kept on each dog. They are available for questions, and provide entry forms for future shows. They also provide catalogs which list, by breed and class, each dog that is available for sale to the exhibitors by the hosting kennel club.

A representative of the AKC is present at all sanctioned shows to answer questions and to see that the rules and regulations are adhered to. He observes and grades new judges' performance and assists all judges when questions arise. His primary responsibility is to insure that the show runs smoothly by acting as a liaison to the exhibitors, judges, host club, and superintendent.

The playing field is ready. Referees and field judges are in place. Now let the games begin!

A dog show is an elimination contest, similar to a ladder in a tennis tournament. All competition begins in the breed classes and then proceeds into one of seven groups, each containing several breeds, and culminates in Best in Show which selects the best dog from the winners of each group. During the transition from the breed to the group, Dachshunds have an advantage. Most breeds only have one dog that may advance to group competition.

Three great ladies of the breed—Dorothy Hardy handling Ch. Roderick v.d. Nidda, Nancy Onthank (Dee Hutchinson's Mother) judging, and Roderick's breeder-owner, Mrs. Thassilo von Nidda. Photo by Shafer.

Dachshunds have three varieties within the breed and therefore have one smooth, one wire, and one longhair represented in the group.

The primary motivation of each exhibitor is to make his dog a Champion within the breed. Winning or placements in Group competition, and even Best in Show, is secondary. Once a dog has achieved the title of Champion, it may only be entered in the Best of Breed competition. Outstanding representatives of each breed are often entered in numerous shows with the intent of winning group placements and Best in Shows.

If you are accomplished at reading and ordering from a Chinese menu, then understanding and indulging in dog shows should be as easy for you as deciding on Szechwan shrimp, chicken lo mein, dim sum, or moo goo gai pan. If you are strictly a meat and potatoes person, the learning curve may be more gradual. There are five classes established for each variety and each sex (dog or bitch) in which you may enter your Dachshund. Some classes are limited by your dog's age, size (Miniature or Standard), and breeding. However, you often have a choice.

Following is a list and brief description of each class. It is important to mention that no dogs who have earned the title of Champion are eligible to compete in any of these classes.

Puppy

The Puppy class is limited to dogs that are six to twelve months of age. When there is a large entry, the class may be divided into age groups, six to nine, and nine to twelve months respectively. Miniatures and Standards compete together in this class.

Ch. Venture of Hardway and Am. Can. & Berm. Ch. Herthwood's Mark of Rose Farm, Venture's son, a BIS winner, both owned by Nancy Onthank.

Bred-by-Exhibitor

This class has no size or age limitations other than the minimum age requirement of six months, but is restricted to Dachshunds owned and bred by the exhibitor and shown by the breeder, or a member of the immediate family, including husband, wife, mother, father, son, daughter, brother, or sister. If you did not breed the dog to be shown, then you may not enter this class.

The American Bred

The American Bred class also has no size or age restriction. It is, however, restricted to those dogs bred and whelped in the United States.

Open

The Open class is for any dog six months of age or older that has not completed his championship. In Dachshunds, this class is separated into Miniature and Standard, and in the case of large specialty shows, by color. To enter the Open Miniature class, the dog must be a Miniature twelve months or older and weigh under eleven pounds.

Novice

If you are new to dog shows, then your best choice will be the Novice class. Generally, both the dog and the handler have little or no experience, so it's a good place to start. Your dog must be at least six moths of age, and not have won more than three first prizes in this class in prior shows. Additionally, he may not have won a first prize in Bred-by-Exhibitor, American Bred, or Open, and may not have any points towards his championship.

The winner of each of these classes advances to the Winners classes. Males compete for Winners Dog and females for Winners Bitch. The dog or bitch that placed second to the winners of the Winners class originally returns to the ring to compete for Reserve Winners.

All that remains is Best of Breed. Each variety in the Best of Breed competition brings together already recognized AKC Champions of either sex (specials), plus the Winners Dog and Winners Bitch from the class competition. The judge then selects one from this group as Best of Variety. If the winner is a dog, the judge then selects a bitch for Best of Opposite Sex, and visa versa. If the Winners Dog or Winners Bitch is not selected as Best of Variety, the judge chooses either the dog or the bitch as Best of Winners.

This procedure takes place identically for every breed entered in the show. Each Best of Breed winner competes against all other breed winners in their respective groups, which for Dachshunds is the Hound Group. The winners of each of the seven groups (namely Sporting Dogs, Hounds, Working Dogs, Terriers, Toys, Non-Sporting Dogs, and Herding Dogs) then compete for Best in Show.

Although these procedures appear complicated and competitive, you will be happy to learn that your Dachshund can earn the title of Champion without ever having to win Best of Variety within the breed. Many dogs have earned their championship without ever competing in group competition.

Scene from the Walt Disney film *The Ugly Dachshund*, G.B. Sterne's classic story of a Great Dane that believed himself to be a Dachshund.

To become a Champion, a dog must accumulate a total of fifteen championship points. Points are awarded only by placing first as Winners Dog or Winners Bitch. The amount of points won at a show will vary depending upon both the number of Dachshunds entered and the region of the country in which the show is taking place. A dog who wins one point in fifteen appearances does not meet the criteria for Champion. He must win at least two "majors" of three, four, or five points each, dependent on region and minimum number of dogs competing (not entered) as determined by the AKC. Each major must be under a different judge. This is necessary to insure that a dog must win against sufficient competition.

The country is broken down into several divisions. Points to be awarded for each breed within each division are established annually by the AKC based on number of registrations and prior show entries for that area. All dog show catalogs are required to print the scale of points for all breeds in the region of the country where the show is held. For illustrative purposes, we present the following schedule of points for Dachshunds, which became effective for Division 9 (State of California) on May 17, 1994.

MAJOR

	Number of Points	1	2		3	4	5
Longhaired							
Dogs	Number Competing	2	6		10	15	25
Bitches		2	5		9	14	23
Smooth							
Dogs		2	5		8	12	18
Bitches		2	6		10	15	24
Wirehaired							
Dogs		2	4		7	9	12
Bitches		2	5		9	14	22

There are two exceptions to this schedule of points. Let's assume that you have won Winners Dog in longhairs, but there were only two males competing. According to this schedule your dog is entitled to 1 point, which does not constitute a major. The Winners Bitch having competed against 23 other females is entitled to 5 points and a major. If your dog beats the bitch in the Best of Winners competition, you are entitled to the same award as the bitch (a major and 5 points), instead of the 1 point. The bitch, however, still receives a major and 5 points.

There is one other exception. If your dog is fortunate enough to win Best of Variety, and then goes on to win first in the Hound Group, he is entitled to the maximum number of points awarded to any other dog in the group.

If you think that your Dachshund may be of show quality and you want to enter a dog show, any national dog magazine will list upcoming shows, dates, superintendents, and one or more of the sponsoring club's officers and their addresses. Write for entry blanks and premium lists.

Now that you are familiar with the complexity and competitiveness of dog shows, perhaps you have changed your mind about showing your Dachshund. We hope that it is now clear how serious dog showing really is. Still, if the breeder of your dog thinks he may be of show quality, then by all means test the waters and have fun!

One other type of dog show is worth considering in order to test the waters. In fact, we would encourage you to participate if you want to learn more about your dog, the breed, and others involved with the sport. Most all local kennel clubs have one or more "Match Shows" during the year. These may be sanctioned and governed by the rules of the AKC, or may be just "fun" matches where anything goes. Judges may be licensed by the AKC, but are not required to be, and more often than not, they are just breeders or aspiring judges. Generally, entries are restricted to dogs who have not been awarded championship points and who are at least three months old. No points are awarded, but ribbons and prizes are bestowed upon the winners. Rarely will any professional handlers be present. Most are breeders or owners of dogs who use the forum as a training ground for their young dogs. Winning is unimportant, and all participants—both canine and human—just relax and enjoy the day. It's a great opportunity to talk, ask questions, learn, and meet people with similar interests.

Dachshund breeders and owners will be the first to welcome you to a show, and they will encourage your participation. But hopefully, you have a better understanding of what to expect and some of the pitfalls to be overcome. Showing necessitates involvement and commitment, and is not to be taken lightly. Above all, it is a sport. You will lose when you think you should have won, and you will win when you least expect it. You must accept winning with humility and losing with graciousness. Throughout, the

Ch. Double SS My Kind of Town, owned by Shirley Silagi. The only Miniature smooth to win an all breed Best in Show to date.

watchword is patience. The competitors you will come to respect exhibit these characteristics. Others will be noticed, but not remembered.

We never cease to be amazed by the number of calls we receive from people who want to breed their male Dachshund requesting information on how to go about finding a bitch. Our answer is two-fold and always the same, "Don't" and "You won't find one." As much as many men would like to believe otherwise, there are not many women out there just waiting for a stud. As sex turns innocent youth into macho mania in men, so it will with dogs. Once learned, it is not forgotten, and shouldn't be encouraged, unless of course you want a forever-aroused dog lifting his leg on your furniture to mark his territory. There are already too many unwanted dogs in animal shelters, and the burden is on breeders and pet owners alike through responsible breeding practices to minimize this problem. Suffice it to say that unless the breeder of your male Dachshund has specifically requested to breed to him in the future, you will not find a responsible breeder who will arbitrarily breed to your dog.

Unless you bought your bitch with the intent to breed her and discussed this with the breeder at the time of purchase, we will again try to discourage you. If you have already made up your mind to do so, be prepared to pay a stud fee which can amount to several hundred dollars, or expect to relinquish one or more of the best puppies to the owner of the stud. Smaller breeds such as the Dachshund often have birthing problems which can result in a Caesarean Section, and occasionally death. Litter sizes tend to be small, particularly in the Miniatures. Add this to the cost of food, inoculations, and wormings, and your odds of making money are remote.

If you are lucky enough to raise a successful litter, you will then have to see to it that the puppies find their way to good homes. This is often a difficult task even among experienced breeders. When you are dealing in livestock, Murphy's law always applies, and can even be expanded. Things can, do, and will go wrong sooner or later. You must be prepared for this eventuality and be ready to deal with the heartache, expense, and the risk.

chapter 10

Obedience

Webster defines obedient as "obeying or willing to obey." In the canine world, Obedience has two connotations: training your Dachshund to be obedient in the home and training for Obedience in the competitive environment of Obedience Trials. Both will be discussed.

In recent years, training your new puppy in a "classroom" environment has enjoyed increasing popularity, and where best to begin? Why kindergarten, of course.

As the name implies, Kindergarten Puppy Training is very much the same concept as for children: the beginning of structured learning for the very young. A popular misconception among many dog owners is that a dog cannot learn in this way until he reaches the magic age of six months, and yet nobody would think of delaying the schooling process of a normal child until he is on the threshold of adolescence. In fact, puppies can and do learn prior to six months—often learning things we would prefer they had not. Wouldn't it be nice to write on that innocent little pup's slate before he gets it all scribbled up with things we will later have to erase? Well, one of the primary purposes of KPT is to do just that. By seven weeks of age a puppy's brain is fully able to learn, although his span of attention is demonstrably shorter than that of a mature dog. On the plus side, however, is the fact that his attitude about human authority is still in the formative stage.

Up until about four months of age, your dog is like a wet piece of clay that you have the opportunity to mold into whatever you desire. What your puppy learns and is exposed to during this crucial time lays the foundation for everything from simple companionship to his future in Obedience Trials and the breed ring. This is the stage when a puppy's attitude towards other dogs and the surrounding world is most profoundly shaped—it is crucial to use this time to shape your dog's personality, as it is not something you can go back and do later. If you don't do it at this point, the puppy will never be the obedient dog that he might have become if he had gotten this all-important early attention. The training is needed on an individual level, not as a member of a litter in "pack" activities.

The exercises that we teach our puppies in class are essentially those that are taught in a regular "adult" Obedience class, but they are tailored to a pup's short attention span. We also take into account a dog's playful attitude towards his classmates. During the frequent brakes for "recess," the puppies can engage in playful antics (on leash, of course) with each other. This naturally could not be allowed in a class of adult dogs. The very large and the very small learn how to behave appropriately with each other; the timid puppy gains self-confidence, and the overly assertive puppy is taught restraint. Puppies who do not live in households with children or men, or are not exposed much to strangers generally have the opportunity to become acquainted with these types of people in a non-threatening atmosphere at puppy class. Even the car ride en route to puppy class is a valuable experience for the young puppy. All puppies will profit from this early socialization outside of their familiar surroundings, but for some it will literally mean the difference between whether they develop into neurotic and fearful or confident and outgoing adults.

We feel that puppies should come into puppy class at about ten to twelve weeks of age and not be accepted once they are over four and a half months unless the circumstances are unusual. For one thing, a puppy's attitude towards human authority can still be turned around if necessary, and it is truly amazing how many owners are, at this stage, already well on their way to abdicating their rightful position as "pack leader" to the puppy. It is perfectly normal for a puppy to try to improve his position in the "pack" (his human family), but in a canine pack, he would also be put in his place. His human "pack leader" needs to know how to do this.

We think that the most exciting feature of Kindergarten Puppy Training is the fact that the puppies themselves are so receptive to your teachings at this age. Experience with our own dogs, that began their education in various areas at this stage, has proved that their very aptitude for learning itself seems to be increased. Certainly their attitude towards any kind of training is a decidedly positive one. Comparing our dogs of today who have had the benefit of KPT classes as youngsters, with those we trained in the past the "old-fashioned way" (beginning their class training at six months of age or older), we are convinced that those who had KPT actually have greater potential and learn faster than their traditionally trained counterparts. It gives the puppy a head start, and from the standpoint of the owner, anything a puppy does right is wonderful, so the training atmosphere itself is a very positive and rewarding cycle.

"Well, if you're really serious about Obedience training, get a Border Collie or a Golden Retriever; they're the smartest." How many times have we fans of the short folk heard statements like that directed towards us? Often the speaker will expand upon this advice with further declarations of the breeds of dogs that are the "most intelligent." One recent publication, which drew wide attention, featured an extensive list of breeds in supposed order of intelligence. Not surprisingly, Dachshunds ranked pretty far down the line—about 89th, but just as beauty is often in the eye of the beholder, determining how smart a dog is depends on what "yard stick" you are using. Is the dog, for example, quick and responsive to taking directions and learning routines, or is he a problem-solver who invariably manages to escape from any enclosure in which you try to contain him, stubbornly pursuing the objective until it is successful? Intelligence manifests itself in many forms. It seems that our concept of the nature of intelligence needs further development, rather than intelligence itself.

Dogs generally come in an extraordinary variety of shapes, sizes, abilities, and inclinations. All purebreds were developed by man at some point for a specific purpose. Some were used to hunt, others to look after livestock, guard property, eradicate vermin, and so on. In the course of shaping desirable characteristics, the original architects of those evolving breeds selectively bred for physical and behavioral traits that rendered the dog best suited for the task at hand. Dogs became specialists, so to speak, rather than all-arounders. Knowing what a given breed was originally intended to do will offer considerable insight into the nature of the beast—in short, what makes it tick.

While all dogs share certain behavioral characteristics, those which were brought into sharper focus to "custom design" a breed for a particular line of work will clue you in when determining what that dog is like to train and live with in general. Dachshunds are known for the physical adaptations and gutsy never-give-up attitude that makes them so ideally suited for going to the ground after such daunting prey as badgers. It shouldn't come as any surprise then, that if you should find yourself in a battle of wills with a Dachshund you will not be envied.

In training any dog, but especially one with this kind of personality, we believe that it is preferable to use an inductive rather than a forceful approach. A dog will adopt behavior that results in reward. If you know of something a dog enjoys, you already have a key to unlocking his desire to please you. Toys and games of fetch might be a powerful motive for the Golden Retriever, but they will leave a Dachshund cold (although we do have one feisty little bitch that loves nothing better than to, after a training session, tear after a floppy toy and thoroughly "kill it" before bearing it proudly back to me for another toss.) For the actual training however, I have rarely seen a Dachshund that didn't turn on for food as if each tid-bit was all that stood between him and starvation.

If you want to teach your puppy to sit on command you could simply give him the command, gently placing him in the desired position, then praising

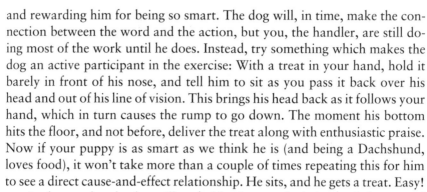

and rewarding him for being so smart. The dog will, in time, make the connection between the word and the action, but you, the handler, are still doing most of the work until he does. Instead, try something which makes the dog an active participant in the exercise: With a treat in your hand, hold it barely in front of his nose, and tell him to sit as you pass it back over his head and out of his line of vision. This brings his head back as it follows your hand, which in turn causes the rump to go down. The moment his bottom hits the floor, and not before, deliver the treat along with enthusiastic praise. Now if your puppy is as smart as we think he is (and being a Dachshund, loves food), it won't take more than a couple of times repeating this for him to see a direct cause-and-effect relationship. He sits, and he gets a treat. Easy!

In short order, the dog will probably give you the behavior in hopes and anticipation that you will give him a goodie. By giving your Dachshund a vested interest in this activity, you have certainly secured his cooperation, at least for the moment. Short, happy training sessions that end while your puppy is still eager for more will yield the best results in the long run.

Ever notice how easy it is to teach a Dachshund to beg? Some don't even need to be taught. I have one young male who wouldn't know what I meant if I asked him verbally to "beg pretty," which the older dogs all readily respond to, but he has taken note of the fact that when they do beg, attention and treats are often the result. So, as the adage goes, "monkey see, monkey do." In this case, he has taught *himself* that charming trick. It certainly pays dividends as far as he is concerned. Dogs who perform so-called parlor tricks usually get lots of positive feedback as a result (both literally and figuratively). This is what motivates them to learn and repeat the behavior in the first place. Everyone thinks they're cute and wonderfully clever. I think it is important to remember that when setting out to teach even more advanced and complex training exercises, one way or another, there has got to be something in it for the dog too.

In case you are beginning to think that this business of food rewards is destined to turn your Dachshund into a performing seal—willing to work only as long as the goodies are forthcoming—I can tell you I have not found that to be the case. Certainly the food does act as a powerful incentive to learn the desired behavior to begin with, but since you are going to be petting and praising him verbally for his efforts as well, he is also learning how extremely pleasant it can be to please you generally. Moreover, as his consistency and understanding of the exercise grows, you will not be giving him a tid-bit every time, but since you do still reward him with a well-timed treat at various intervals during training, he is never quite sure that one won't be offered at any moment.

Be creative, and think like a Dachshund! By the time you are undertaking to teach him more complex exercises, you undoubtedly have a pretty good idea of what trips his trigger. Timing is crucial, but we figure that if we can manipulate our dog by almost any means to perform the desired behavior even *once,* and immediately praise him to the skies, we just may have taken a quantum leap towards showing him what we want him to do. If we can make it really worth his while to follow through and do it repeatedly, we have made him our partner and harnessed that same never-say-die tenacity which some merely see as stubbornness.

Of course, sooner or later it becomes necessary to deliver a well timed correction. In the beginning, we do everything possible to have the dog under the kind of control (on a leash or a flexie) where it is virtually impossible for him to make a mistake in the first place. This allows him to give a successful response, and me to give him lots of legitimately earned praise. Praise is a far more potent training tool than correction in this context. For correction to have a positive effect at the learning stage, it must be delivered at the very moment the infraction is taking place, followed immediately by showing the dog what you *do* want. Thus, if my dog is supposed to be doing a Sit-Stay for example, and he starts to move out of that position, I move in to correct him as he is in the act of moving, popping the leash upwards and commanding, "No, Sit" in a firm voice, and praising him for returning to the correct position, "Good Sit." If you have gotten good at "reading your dog" you might even be able to catch him in mid-thought as he is about to move. Here a verbal "Ah-Ha! . . . Sit!" reminder can sometimes be useful, especially on a soft dog. The more we can set the dog up for success, the more productive the training session is going to be. If we do run into a snag, we feel it is imperative to end on a happy note with something the dog can do well and receive praise for. During the proofing stages, this will probably be an easier version of the exercise in question, backing up to a level where he was consistently successful. However, if we're really in a snarl, we may simply finish with something so easy and upbeat at which we know he will succeed. The only situation in which we might feel justified in administering a punitive correction is when we are absolutely certain that the dog understood what we wanted him to do and had no legitimate reason for refusing to comply. In such circumstances, he will understand why he is suffering the consequences. Our dogs so rarely try to beat the system in this way that we are far more inclined to give them the benefit of the doubt and assume that a mistake is an honest one. On the few occasions when we have known otherwise, we truly believe that the offender recognized the fairness of the resulting discipline.

Dachshunds have the potential to be bright, highly motivated Obedience dogs. However, they are not little robots programmed with computer chips, and because they are so intelligent it is essential to keep them feeling both challenged and rewarded by their training sessions. As mentioned earlier, short, happy lessons are usually the most productive. (After all, you don't want your dog to become bored by excessive repetition and start improvising on his own). Just as large triumphs are composed of many small successes, advanced training levels are built from a succession of simpler skills. The perfection with which a dog performs the most complicated exercise is directly linked to the care his trainer has taken in teaching its smaller components. What a Dachshund can learn from an imaginative and dedicated trainer is virtually limitless.

Although there are many excellent dog training books and tapes available which are very useful, an Obedience class conducted by a qualified instructor is highly recommended. It will help keep you motivated too. For information on reputable trainers and Obedience clubs in your area, we recommend that you contact your local kennel club. Please note that the operative word here is *reputable*. In most parts of the country there is very little to keep virtually anyone who wishes to from hanging out her shingle and proclaiming herself a dog trainer. So, choose your training instructors with the same scrutiny you would employ if you were selecting a day care center for your children. If your area has a Dachshund club, or you happen to know someone who shows in Obedience, that's a good place to start. The kind of instructor you are looking for is someone who has trained and attained advanced Obedience degrees on her own dogs. If you attend dog shows in your area (which include Obedience Trials), talk to the handlers of dogs whose attitude and ring performance impressed you. Pay special attention to those who exhibit the more unusual breeds, which may present more of a challenge to train. Ask where they train or whom they might recommend. Once you and your Dachshund become involved in the world of dog training, you may just find yourself thoroughly hooked on a captivating sport. At the very least you will gain insight into the art of communicating with your short-legged friend, who in turn will be a more enjoyable companion.

Ch. Ivic's Advance Notice, CDX, TD, CG, VC and DAM. Ch. Ivic Cevan's Chimney Sweep, VDT, owned by Jane Larsen. *Photo by Bob Brownback.*

As almost any dog lover who attends dog shows will readily attest, the highest level of spectator interest will usually be found around the Obedience rings. The appeal is obvious: People can watch dogs performing structured training routines at various levels of difficulty, which are nevertheless pretty readily understood by anyone. The AKC offers Obedience competition at three different levels, ranging from Novice through Open and Utility. The order is progressive—a dog must earn one title before competing for the next. For each title, this is done by earning a qualifying score at three separate trials under three different judges. These qualifying scores are referred to as "legs" (a curious terminology since a dog requires only three of them to be awarded the title in question). To quote the AKC Obedience Regulations, "A qualifying score shall be comprised of scores of more than 50% of the available points in each exercise and a final score of 170 or more points, earned in a single Regular class at a Licensed or Member Obedience Trial . . ." Without getting into a detailed discussion of the fine points of scoring itself, suffice it to say that it is based on the premise that a dog and handler enter the ring with a perfect score of 200 points. As the two progress through their routine, deductions may be taken from this for imperfections in the performance.

NOVICE

A dog who has satisfied the requirements for a Novice title is entitled to put the letters "C.D." (Companion Dog) after his name. In the Novice Ring, each dog and handler team will perform four individual exercises, in sequence, at the judge's direction. They will also participate in two group exercises with other dogs and handlers from the class.

Heel on Leash & Figure Eight

The judge will direct the handler, with his dog in the heel position on his left side, to walk a predetermined pattern in the ring. Typically, this is often an L-shaped pattern, but the judge will, in any event, choose a sequence of commands which serves to illustrate the pair's ability to smoothly execute changes of pace (normal, fast, and slow) as well as left turn, right turn, about-turn, and halts. The figure eight portion of the exercise is conducted around two ring stewards with the judge calling starts and stops. Here, however, the handler is to maintain a consistent pace, and it is up to the dog to speed up or slow down as the two maneuver their way around the "posts." Skillfully performed, this appears natural and easy, but in reality it represents a great deal of work and cooperation from both of the partners. A truly superior Heeling exhibition is poetry in motion and a joy to watch. If you doubt the degree of difficulty involved, just try keeping in step with a human companion who is changing speeds and directions without informing you as she goes along.

Heeling is one Obedience activity which the handler and dog will continue to fine tune throughout their career, for it has numerous applications all the way up the line. It is also the first exercise that the judge will see the two perform when they come under her scrutiny in the ring.

Stand for Examination

This exercise is fairly self-explanatory, and consists of the handler placing the dog in a comfortable stance, walking six feet out in front of him to stand quietly facing the dog while the judge walks up and examines the animal. This is done off leash, and the dog is not to show shyness or resentment of any kind, or move out of the position in which he was left. The examination itself is essentially a token one since it consists of the judge simply touching the dog on his head, body, and hindquarters with the fingers and palm of one hand. She then directs the handler to return to the heel position and declares, "Exercise finished." The point of the exercise is for the dog to exhibit a willingness to stay where he is placed (a short distance from the handler), and allow a stranger to touch him. One might argue that it is a test of both training and stable temperament. The exercise is conducted in such a predictable and virtually choreographed style that the majority of dogs become comfortable with the procedure in a ring setting. The exercise frequently seems to offer a peculiar kind of challenge to Dachshunds, however, in view of their tendency to adopt a sort of "second gear squat" position which is neither a stand or a sit. Confidence and a clear understanding on the part of the dog concerning exactly what position is desired are critically important. While these are in the process of being firmly established, patience is essential on the part of an often frustrated trainer. Don't be led down the garden path by the sympathetic observations of non-Dachshund friends who exclaim, "But the poor little fellow is so close to the ground anyway, how can you tell what he is doing?"

Heel Free

This exercise, as the name implies, is done off leash and involves the same heeling pattern as the one done previously on leash. In this case, however, the figure eight is eliminated. A number of dogs actually score better on their off-lead exercise than the one done on lead; the leash after all, is another element to contend with in executing a smooth performance. However, a dog who lacks sufficient training and attention to his handler is very likely to become quite lost or confused without the restrictive influence of that connecting leash, and as a result, fail.

Recall

As any Obedience instructor will undoubtedly confirm, the most frequently voiced request by a dog owner is, "I want my dog to come when I call him!"

The recall exercise is designed to illustrate that control. On order from the judge, the handler leaves the dog at one end of the ring, proceeds to the opposite end, and then calls him when told to do so. If the dog has correctly learned his part, he will come eagerly in to his handler (close enough to be easily touched), and sit straight in front of him. Finally, at the judge's direction, the handler commands the dog to go to the heel position once again. The dog may either go to the right or the left of his handler. It is not uncommon for trainers to teach their dogs both routes, utilizing different commands to distinguish between the two.

For the trainer who wishes to score well throughout all levels of Obedience competition, the importance of straight fronts (the part of an exercise where a dog comes in and sits in front of his handler), and finishes (where he goes to and sits smartly beside the handler in the heel position) cannot be overestimated. I suspect that more time and creativity are expended on perfecting these two elements than almost any other skills. As simple as these two things may appear to be on the surface, they can make an enormous difference in a dog's total score, depending on whether they are executed sloppily or with precision.

The group exercises are conducted in batches of six to twelve dogs after the participants have finished being judged on their own individual exercises. A ring steward will lead the handlers with their dogs on leash into the ring in catalog order and space them along one side, making sure that each pair has adequate space between themselves and the pairs to either side. Armbands and leashes are then detached and placed behind the dogs. Upon order from the judge, the handlers will all sit their dogs, tell them to stay, and proceed to the opposite side of the ring where they stand quietly, facing their dogs. After one minute (which can feel like at least an hour to a nervous handler) has elapsed the judge orders the handlers return to their respective dogs, circling behind them, and arriving back beside them in the heel position. When everyone has gotten back to his or her dog, the judge will tell the group, "Exercise finished," concluding the Long Sit exercise. The Long Down is conducted in the same manner except that in this instance the dogs are commanded to lie down and are left in position for three minutes. While being judged the dogs must not move from the position in which they were left or cause any kind of a disturbance. At the conclusion of each batch of group exercises, the judge will go down the line of exhibitors and tell each one whether or not he has qualified (received a qualifying score). Even a dog who has flunked one of his earlier exercises is expected to show up and participate in the group exercises.

It may seem that we have placed a disproportionate amount of emphasis on the importance of the Novice exercises, but they form the basic foundation for what lies ahead at higher levels of training. If that foundation has been built upon proverbial sand, it is going to suffer structural weaknesses later on which will be more difficult to correct.

OPEN

The next rung on the ladder of Obedience competition is the Open A class for dogs seeking their Companion Dog Excellent (C.D.X.) titles.

Sometimes referred to as "the heartbreak class," there is actually quite a gap between the percentage of qualifiers coming out of the average Novice class at a show and that yielded by the Open A class. Once a dog has earned his C.D., he is no longer eligible to compete at that level. A non-regular class called the Graduate Novice Class is offered at Obedience Trials. This class involves no jumping or retrieving, and is available only to dogs with a C.D. who have not yet earned a qualifying score towards their C.D.X. It's sort of a "not yet ready for prime-time" kind of class in which a dog can continue to gain ring experience and compete for ribbons while not advancing towards any title.

In the Open class, all exercises are performed off-lead, and the first thing each exhibitor is asked as she enters the show ring is to relinquish the leash to the steward and stand the dog so that the dog's height at the withers can be measured by the judge. Dachshunds are one of those breeds for which the AKC Obedience Regulations have wisely decreed that their High Jump ". . . shall be set at the nearest multiple of 2 inches to the height of the dog at the withers or 8 inches, whichever is greater. . ." The Broad Jump is then twice whatever the measurement of the High Jump is figured to be.

As in the Novice class, the first exercise in Open is the Heel with a figure eight—only this is done off-lead. Ironically, many dogs who have been concentrating on the new "harder" exercises will do surprisingly poorly here.

Next comes the Drop on Recall exercise, identical to the Novice Recall but with one critical difference—the handler, on the judge's signal, must drop

Longhair Mini doing the broad jump—a long low jump for a long, low dog.

the dog midway after calling him to come in. The dog must drop to the floor on command and remain there until called in to complete the remainder of the Recall. There are a great many possible pitfalls that can cause a dog to fail this exercise. A delicate balance must be maintained between keeping the enthusiastic drive of a dog eager to reach his handler (before and after the drop), and the kind of control which enables the handler to drop him mid-stride.

Next comes the Retrieve on Flat exercise wherein the handler, at the judge's direction, tells her dog to wait, throws the dumbbell, sends the dog after it, takes the dumbbell when it is delivered to hand, and then, finally, sends the dog to heel. A dog that has been taught to do straight Fronts from any direction will have a significant advantage executing any of the retrieving exercises, since he may frequently find it necessary to approach from an angle. But, it is teaching the dog to retrieve on command in the first place which all too commonly proves to be the stumbling block that keeps owners from taking their dogs on into Open competition. The fact that a dog delights in retrieving toys in play, pouncing enthusiastically on his prize and "killing it" before proudly returning with it may have little connection with teaching him a formal Obedience retrieve. The latter is the result of carefully assembled parts of the exercise so that the dog not only understands exactly what is being asked of him, but also that he does not have the option to refuse.

The Retrieve Over High Jump exercise is essentially the same as the one done on the flat except that the dog must go out and back over the jump. Here again, a dog that has received adequate proofing on this exercise will

"Come and sit!" The successful return with the dumbbell.

Standard wire with dumb-
bell.

be more likely to come back over the jump with the dumbbell, even if his
handler has made a "bad toss" causing it to bounce off to one side where it
is tempting for the dog to return past the jump by the most direct route. As
stated earlier, the Broad Jump measures twice the distance of the High Jump.
For a Dachshund, this obstacle will consist of two broad jump boards evenly
spaced so that they total the proper number of inches lengthwise that the dog
is to jump. After leaving her dog at least eight feet back from the jump, the
handler positions herself, facing the right side of the jump, and when told to
do so, calls her dog over it. The temptation to "walk the jump" rather than
go through the effort of clearing it, is strong for some dogs (after all, we can't
really explain to a dog that we are pretending the boards are something that
he can't navigate on foot such as a body of water). When the dog is in mid-
air over the jump, the handler executes a right-angle turn, so that she is facing the same direction from which the dog is jumping. The exercise is then
completed with a conventional Front and Finish at the judge's order. If not
carefully taught, there is a considerable tendency on the part of most dogs to
"cut the corner" of the Broad Jump in an effort to reach the handler via the
shortest possible route. Like so many other aspects of the teaching process, if
the handler has taken short cuts in training, she may eventually find her dog
taking short cuts with an exercise in the ring.

The Long Sit and Long Down Group exercises are conducted in a similar manner to the ones in Novice except that they are even longer (a three
minute Sit and a five minute Down). This time the handlers don't just go across
the ring—now they go out of sight! A ring steward leads the handlers out of
the ring, and to a location (often completely outside the building if the show
is held indoors) where the dogs are unaware of their presence. Here, the har-
ried handlers bide their time checking their watches, chewing their nails, and
anxiously imagining all kinds of disasters which might be occurring in their
absence. If you should cross paths with a line of grim faced individuals, arms
akimbo, headed purposefully in some direction at a show, they are probably

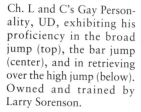

Ch. L and C's Gay Personality, UD, exhibiting his proficiency in the broad jump (top), the bar jump (center), and in retrieving over the high jump (below). Owned and trained by Larry Sorenson.

Open class handlers. If they look as if they are headed to an execution, they are undoubtedly exiting the ring. On the other hand, if they appear to be in an exceptional hurry, get out of their way—they're making their return trip and likely to mow down anything in their paths in their haste to get back and reassure themselves that all is well!

UTILITY

If one were to compare the three basic levels of Obedience Competition to our educational system, with Novice and Open being comparable to grade-school and high school respectively, then Utility is certainly college. The exercises themselves are more complex and demand more of the dog's total attention to his handler. The importance of having instilled superior training skills at the most basic levels soon becomes apparent. Moreover, a special degree of confidence on the dog's part is required if he is to succeed in Utility, because the majority of things he will be asked to do involve choices. For instance, it is no longer simply a matter of going out and promptly retrieving an item for his handler on command; now he will also need to know which is the correct one to bring back. Anyone who has ever experienced that hollow feeling in the pit of his stomach at the fear that he may not know the right answer to the teacher's question can readily appreciate the stress potential here.

Over the years there have been more changes in the evolution of Utility than in those in either Novice or Open classes. In Canada, these first two levels are essentially the same as those offered here by the AKC. The Utility classes in the two countries now differ substantially however, so a dog that has earned a U.D. title from both the CKC and the AKC has mastered quite an array of different routines.

In Open, the dog performed his Heeling routine off leash. The *Signal Exercise* in Utility adds still another level of difficulty to this activity: it is done entirely on hand signals with no spoken commands by the handler permitted. To quote from the AKC Regulations, "The principal features of this exercise are the ability of the dog and handler to work as a team while heeling, and the dog's correct responses to the signals to Stand, Drop, Sit, and Come." Initially the exercise involves the kind of heeling pattern commonly seen in the Novice or Open. Then, when the pair reaches one end of the ring at a normal pace the judge will command, "Stand your dog." The handler pauses long enough to do this, tells the dog to stay, walks to the opposite end of the ring, and faces him. The judge is now positioned behind the standing dog, out of his line of vision. From this vantage point she can observe both parties as she gestures silently to the handler to drop the dog from a stand, sit him from the dropped position, call him in, and finally to go from the front to the heel position. There is an obvious chain of command here which must be promptly reacted to, but never anticipated, by either the handler or the dog. Other than variations in the heeling pattern itself, the entire exercise is completely standardized and the changes of position are always performed in the exact same sequence. However, an inattentive or easily distracted dog runs the risk of missing a signal. Ironically, an insecure dog may sometimes seem to seek refuge in this very fact—almost as if he has decided that a sin of omission (failing to respond to the signal because he didn't see it in the first place) is preferable to one of commission (giving the wrong response to a signal). It should be remembered that the above described routine is actually made up of many carefully and independently taught responses, and that a dog does not think in the abstract.

Teach him to sit from a standing position, and you will still have to show your dog what you want when you ask him to assume that position from a down.

Scent Discrimination

An Obedience exhibitor once remarked that the higher the level of training you aspire to, the more stuff you must haul around! Well, Utility certainly does involve bringing more equipment to the ring, and one such necessity is a set of what are known as scent articles. There are actually two sets, one of five identical leather articles not more than six inches in length, and another of metal ones, but together they comprise the full set used in the ring. The majority of these are probably commercially made for training and competition purposes, but over the years we have seen an intriguing variety of home-made versions (which are also perfectly acceptable as long as they meet with the judge's approval). Each of these must be legibly numbered as well. Briefly, this exercise is made up of two parts, and designed to show that the dog can select either a metal article or a leather article which the dog's handler has touched (and consequently left his or her scent upon) from among others which have been handled by someone else simply by using his nose. It is certainly a well-established fact that a dog's sense of smell is many more times acute that of humans. A dog acquires vital knowledge about the surrounding world through this favorite sense from the moment he first drew breath and had to blindly root around for the source of his first meal. So, it isn't a question of having taught the dog how to use his nose, but of having successfully conveyed to him how you want him to use it in this context.

There are several popular methods of teaching this exercise, and it is open to debate which is the best. For each trainer the deciding factor is probably what she finds most effective for getting positive results from her dog. In any case, what is most unique about this exercise is that we are seeking to direct and shape something that we, as humans, cannot do ourselves (and don't entirely understand either). We would compare it to one of us being color-blind and faced with the challenge of teaching a child who sees colors clearly to locate a green object reliably on command.

Back to the ring. The ring steward places all but one leather and one metal article in a random scattering on the floor about six inches apart, and twenty feet away from the watching dog and handler. In the process, she has also imparted her scent to these articles. The handler and his dog then turn their backs to the articles and remain facing away from them while the handler first takes one of the two retained articles (either the metal or the leather one), and handles it, now imparting his own scent to it, then relinquishes it to the waiting judge who places it among the others out on the floor. Having done this, the judge then instructs the handler to turn, face the articles once more, and send his dog for the one which now bears his scent. Once the dog has returned with the correct article, delivered it to his handler, and been sent to the heel position, the first half of the exercise is complete. The first article is then set aside, and the remaining one is used in the same way. If the dog has brought back an incorrect article, that one as well as the one he was supposed to fetch are removed for the second portion of the Scent exercise (he has flunked as a result of this error, but is nevertheless allowed to perform the rest of the exercise with one less article on the floor). It is interesting to watch how individual dogs go about searching for the correct article: Some dash out and appear to go almost immediately to the correct one, seizing it and returning without the slightest hesitation. Others methodically check each and every article before coming to a decision. As long as it is clearly working, it is immaterial what a given dog's "style" appears to be. What is sadly nerve-racking is the sight of a dog who goes out and stands over the articles looking utterly lost, as if he would rather be almost anywhere else! It is unlikely that the dog's scenting ability is to blame in such instances, but rather that somewhere along the line, he has become confused about what is wanted, or fearful of the consequences of being wrong. However, the sight of an eager, confident dog working scent articles with dispatch is thrilling to behold.

Directed Retrieve

This exercise undoubtedly had its origins in field work where a dog is sent on a "blind retrieve" in a particular direction for a bird that he cannot see. The Obedience ring version of this is actually pretty artificial looking, but does serve to illustrate the dog's ability to take the line indicated by his handler when other choices are available (once again note the recurring theme of choices). Here, the handler and dog are positioned in the center of the ring, in line with the bar and solid jumps set up on either side to their left and right. As the handler stands with his back to the far end of the ring with his dog sitting in the heel position, the steward drops three white work gloves (also provided by the handler) across the end of the ring, one in each corner, and one in the center. All three gloves will be clearly visible to the dog and handler when the pair turn to face the glove designated by the judge for the dog to retrieve. The gloves are designated "One," "Two," and "Three" from left to right when the handler turns and faces the gloves. The handler must turn in place with his dog still at heel and face the designated glove. "In place" is the key phrase here and precise footwork can make all the difference in whether or not the team "makes a good turn." (The importance of this becomes readily apparent when one realizes that the more accurately the handler has managed to position his dog facing the desired glove, the greater the certainty that he will go directly to it and not be tempted to veer off and bring back one of the other two gloves instead.) To again quote from the AKC Regulations, "The handler will then give his dog the direction to the designated glove with a single motion of his left hand and arm along the right side of the dog, and will give a verbal command to retrieve . . ." For a dog the size of a Dachshund, the handler is permitted to bend his body and knees to the extent necessary to give the direction, after which he will again stand erect in a natural position. This exercise calls for the retrieval of only one of the three gloves, but it must be the "right" one—the one that the judge has requested!

Moving Stand and Examination

This exercise is pretty self-explanatory and easy to understand from the spectator's point of view. Until just recently, Utility also had a Group exercise known as the Group Examination which consisted of dogs being stood by their handlers in a line similar to that in the Group Stays and being gone over, one at a time, by the judge in a manner similar to that seen in the breed ring. Popular opinion held it to be both time consuming and dull for all concerned, and it has now been replaced by the following version:

On orders from the judge, the handler heels his dog in a straight line at a normal pace for about ten feet, at which point the judge will give the command, "Stand your dog." The handler will, without pausing, order his dog to stand, continue forward ten to twelve feet, and turn around to face the dog. (The flawless execution of this portion of the exercise calls for the dog to stop dead in his tracks the moment he is told to do so by his handler, a maneuver which exhibits rather impressive teamwork between the two, as the human partner continues forward at the same brisk pace without hesitation.) The judge then approaches the dog from the front, goes over him, and finally tells the handler to call his dog directly to heel. (It is the one exercise where the dog, returning to his handler, does not first Front before being commanded to Finish, i.e., go to the heel position.) The examination itself is considerably more thorough than that which the Novice contestant submitted to, and closely approximates the one seen in the Breed ring, except that in this instance neither teeth nor testicles are examined. As with the Novice Stand for Exam, the dog must accept the examination without shyness or resentment.

Directed Jumping

This exercise provides the dramatic finale in the Utility class, and is invariably a crowd-pleaser. It is conducted in two parts, and incorporates a couple of distinctly different skills: the Send Away (familiar to field trainers), and the Directed Jumping, where the dog is told which of two jumps to take on the way back to his handler.

It works like this: dog and handler are positioned on the center line at one end of the ring and about twenty feet from the line of jumps (a bar-jump on one side and a high-jump on the other, as described previously). On order from the judge, the handler sends his dog back. Ideally, the dog is supposed to keep going in a straight line until he is stopped by a further command—a distance of at least another twenty feet beyond the jumps. At this point, the dog is to turn and sit facing his handler, waiting for further instruction. The judge then calls out which of the two jumps he wants the dog to take, either "High" or "Bar." The handler, in turn, then commands or signals the dog to take the desired jump, and as he is in mid-air over the jump, he turns so as to be facing the dog as he returns. A normal Front and Finish conclude that portion of the exercise. This is repeated once more in exactly the same manner except that this time the dog will be sent over whichever jump he was not instructed to take in the first instance. (If he has executed all of this correctly and with flair, thunderous applause usually follows!)

Although the jumping element of this exercise is likely to be viewed as the most thrilling, it is often the Send Away portion which offers the greater challenge to trainers. Much ingenuity is spent in developing ways to insure that a dog learns to travel back in as straight a path as possible and does not slow up or stop prematurely. There are, of course, many possible things that can go wrong in the jumping phase as well—a dog may decide to take the "wrong" jump (some dogs seem to prefer one jump over the other). He may knock one of the jumps as he attempts to clear it, be tempted to run under the bar jump, or by-pass either of the jumps altogether. Directed jumping is yet another excellent example of how vital the trainer's careful attention to detail is. (Sometimes, only when the various parts of an exercise begin to disintegrate during a performance do we fully realize how painstaking the assembly was in the first place!)

Once a dog has earned his U.D. (Utility Dog) title, two additional areas of competition are open for him to pursue.

The Obedience Trial Championship (O.T. Ch.) is competitive in the same sense that a breed Champion of Record is—to achieve one, it is necessary to defeat others.

Quoting from the AKC Obedience Regulations, the requirements for an O.T.Ch. are as follows:

1. Shall have won 100 points; and
2. shall have won a first place in utility (or Utility B, if divided) provided there are at least 3 dogs in competition; and
3. shall have won a first place in Open B provided there are at least 6 dogs in competition; and
4. shall have won a third First place under the conditions of 2 or 3 above; and
5. shall have won these three First places under three different judges, at all breed obedience trials, whether held separately or in conjunction with an all breed dog show."

Miniature wires can jump too.

With dumbbell in mouth this Dachshund is successfully over the jump.

Precision and the exceptional performance which result in high scores are obviously of primary consideration if a dog is to succeed in this arena.

The first Dachshund (and also the first member of the Hound Group) to win an Obedience Trial Championship was a Standard longhair bitch, Mayrhofen Olympischer Star L, U.D.T. owned by Kay Thompson. "Gretl" and Kay made their mark in Dachshund history on October 23, 1977 going High in Trial at the Minneapolis K.C. show.

The second Dachshund (and coincidentally the first Dachshund breed Champion of Record to earn the coveted O.T.Ch.), Ch. Himark Vanquish, U.D.T. "Vance," was a Standard longhair dog, owned by Robert and June Kelly. Vance and Rob claimed their Dual Championship on December 12, 1981.

Perhaps it would be pertinent to explain here, too, that reference to a dog's U.D. title is automatically eliminated at the end of his name once he has also earned an O.T.Ch. (Presumably the drafters of such protocol reasoned that since an Obedience Trial Champion must necessarily possess a

Shown with his owner, Robert Kelly, American and Canadian (conformation) and O.T. Ch. Himark Vanquish U.D.T., the first Dachshund bred Champion of record to earn the coveted O.T.C.h.

U.D. title, it would be redundant to indicate it again at the other end of the name.) If a dog has a T.D. (Tracking Dog) title as well as a U.D., this will appear at the end of his name as "U.D.T." However, once the dog has acquired an O.T.Ch., the Tracking title will again be indicated simply by the letters "T.D."

Utility Dog Excellent (U.D.X.) favors a dog who is, above all, capable of delivering consistent qualifying performances. The emphasis here is not so much on high scores as on having the stamina and versatility to do well in both Open and Utility classes at the same trial. In the words of the AKC Regulations, requirements for the Utility Dog Excellent title are as follows:

"1. Shall have earned at ten separate events qualifying scores in both the Open B and Utility B Classes.

2. Shall have earned these qualifying scores at ten Licensed or Member Obedience trials or Dog Shows, provided the sum total of dogs that actually competed in the Open B Class was not less than six, and that the sum total of dogs that actually competed in the Utility Class was not less than three, except that at breed club specialties and at any trial in Puerto Rico, Hawaii or Alaska, qualifying scores will be credited towards the title,

provided the sum total of dogs that actually competed in all of the regular obedience classes is not less than six."

The first Dachshund to earn a Utility Dog Excellent title was a Mini smooth bitch, Ginger Snap Cookie Pindor, U.D., owned by Cindy and Ron Pindor and shown by Cindy.

Dachshunds traditionally succeed in the Obedience environment. They have the commitment, courage, patience, and stamina to do so. The ultimate question is, do you?

chapter 11

The Working Dachshund:
More Than a Lap Dog

While a discussion of any breed always includes the purpose for which the dog was originally bred, most breeds are sadly limited to conformation dog shows, Obedience and Agility Trials, or relegated to their owner's lap. Modern technology and overpopulation have severely restricted man's use of dogs for practical applications. Of course we have exceptions, as several breeds are still actively used for guarding people and property, retrieving, and the herding of animals. Others are used in search and rescue, as guide dogs, and some, such as the racing Greyhound, solely to satisfy some people's desire for entertainment in their leisure time.

The Dachshund thrives on hunting and, if given the opportunity, will spend hours in the fields and woods pursuing game to the point of exhaustion, often forgetting to take the time to eat or drink. While the majority of Dachshunds may never see more than a lap, car, sofa, bed, or occasionally chase a rabbit or squirrel in your back yard, many will experience the exhilaration of the hunt by participating in Den and Field Trials.

With much appreciation to David Kawami for writing the opening segment on Field Trials, and Carrie Hamilton for her contribution of Den Trial History, we present here some viable options for more enjoyment of your Dachshund and your dog's enjoyment of life through participation in activities inherent in the breed. In case you think the Dachshund has outlived its practical usefulness, we think you will be enlightened and fascinated with "Dachshunds In Deer Search," an article by John Jeanneney, which we have reprinted courtesy of *The Dachshund Review*. The article is about a little known and intriguing journey into the world of blood tracking relegated to and reserved primarily for the Dachshund. We have also included a short, but heartwarming and informative essay by Dr. Kit Walter, "Dachshunds as Therapy Dogs."

Lastly, we will discuss the highly debated subject of Dachshund racing. "Racing?" you may ask. "With such short legs, why would anyone be interested in Dachshund racing?" We hope to be able to answer this and other questions concerning this controversial subject.

FIELD TRIALS

What is a Dachshund Field Trial? David Kawami explains:

> For a novice it is important to know that Dachshund Field Trials are bloodless. No game is killed, and the dogs are not encouraged to engage the game. Should the dogs accidentally see the rabbit or hare while they are on the line, the judges generally act quickly to pick up the dogs. The judges are not interested in the Dachshund's ability to sight chase, so what is a Dachshund Field Trial all about?
>
> The Dachshund Field Trial is an adaptation of the Brace Beagle Field Trial in which the dogs track the game. Currently there are three classes that can be entered: Open All Age Dog, Open All Age Bitch, and the non-regular Field Champions. Points toward the AKC Field Champion Title are earned in the open classes. Open All Age means precisely that. All ages are eligible to be entered, as well as Field Champions. It is however, not in the Dachshund's best interest to be started (at Field Trials) too young. Give your Dachshund a chance to mature mentally and emotionally before subjecting him to the pressures of Field Trialing. Nine months to a year is about the right age to begin.

Ch. Ivic's Advance Notice, CDX, TD, CG, VC, shown finding the track layer's glove at trial's end. Photo: Larsen.

The Open Classes are divided by sex, but if there are less than 6 entries in one class the entries are combined. In the early days, a Field Champion may have been entered in the Open Class to reach the 6 entry requirement, thus avoiding a combined class. This rarely happens now, and Field Champions do not participate in the Open Classes.

The Dachshunds are braced (paired) by random draw and assigned a "brace number", brace #1 etc. It is the responsibility of the handlers to be aware of what brace is "down" (being judged) and to be available when their brace is ready to be judged. The Judges will have instructed the Field Marshall on how many braces to bring out to the field (for example, the first four braces). This group, plus any spectators, is referred to as the Gallery. They should remain together, and follow the instructions of the Field Marshall. The Field Marshall will inform the gallery which brace is to be judged.

When the judges are ready, a line of beaters moves through a section of the field trying to move a rabbit from its cover. When a rabbit breaks from cover, the first person to see the rabbit shouts, "TALLY HO!" The judges move to the spot where the rabbit was seen (usually the judges like to "spot," or see their own rabbits in order to more accurately judge the Dachshunds). If they have not seen the rabbit, they ask for an accurate description of where the rabbit went. The brace is "called up." The judges give instructions to the handlers, and the dogs are shown the line (the rabbit scent trail).

The handlers may talk to their dogs and encourage them to find the line. When the dogs indicate that they know where the line is, the handlers

Field Trial—the judges give instructions, the handlers and dogs are shown the line.

The release line is passed through the collar. Drop the rope from one hand and the dog smoothly moves away.

release the Dachshunds. Novice handlers often make the mistake of releasing their dogs too soon.

It takes time and experience to learn when to release your dog. When the dogs are released, the handlers must stop instructing their dogs and end all conversation. They remain behind the judges, and the judges follow the dogs. When the judges have seen enough they will ask that the dogs be picked up. It is now the responsibility of the handlers to find and leash their Dachshunds as quickly as possible. The judges, having discussed the work of the brace, will call the next brace or for another rabbit for the same brace. It is important to listen for the judges' instructions, as not appearing when the judges call for the dogs or bringing the wrong dog to be judged will result in disqualification. The judges allow 15 minutes from the time the brace is called to the time a dog is disqualified for failing to appear. When the judges have called for the next brace, and the judged brace are recovered and leashed, they can rejoin the Gallery, or be taken back to be kenneled. When the handlers have finished running dogs, they are encouraged to join the beaters. There are never enough beaters—and without them and rabbits there is no field trial.

When all the braced Dachshunds have run, the First Series is completed. The judges will confer and decide the Dachshunds who are to be brought back in Second Series. This information will be given to the Field Marshall to be announced. At the conclusion of the Second Series, the judges will again confer and decide which dogs are required for the Third Series. This process will continue until all the places have been determined. The Judges will announce field trial when the Class is completed. (If you would like more information, consult the booklet available from the AKC Registration and field trial rules and Standard Procedures for Dachshunds.)

Dachshund Field Trials can take place in almost any type of weather, often all on the same day. One spring a trial began in four inches of snow, and by noon the snow had stopped. After lunch, most of the snow had melted, and the afternoon was spent in light jackets under a bright sun. There are also the trials that are spent in the rain—six to twelve hours walking around in precipitation varying from mist to driving rain. Trials can also be spent in tee-shirts under a blazing sun. Regardless of the weather, the trial will go on. Sometimes, even in the most severe weather, the Dachshunds, including some minis have a look on their face that says, "What have I done to deserve this?" The human handlers, beaters, and handlers had a similar look. Of course these examples are extremes, and most trials are spent in weather that makes you glad you have the opportunity to be outside. Good, well-fitting boots are absolutely necessary, as you are going to spend at least three hours walking. Jogging shoes can also be worn on dry days—but keep in mind that the trial grounds can be on bottom-land with some swampy areas.

Brush pants or chaps are recommended in some areas of the country. The grounds can have areas of green barbed-wire and multiflora rose. In the North-West, you can look forward to thorn bushes with inch long spikes. Brush pants protect your legs fairly well. A sturdy field jacket to protect your upper body from the thorns and the cold, and a hat to keep the sun and rain off your head are also needed. It is best to layer your clothes, so that you can adjust to weather changes during the day. It is also prudent to bring a change of clothes and shoes. You never know what you may need.

Rain gear, preferably a hooded rain jacket and pants, offers the best protection from wet weather. A rain coat or Poncho will keep your upper body dry, but your lower body will get wet. Wet pants and high rubber boots can lead to some real discomfort; it is possible to develop blisters from the friction of wet pants and boot tops. Well fitting rain boots will save your feet from blisters and keep them dry.

Sunscreen is also necessary—even on overcast days, you can get a good burn. Insect repellent is not usually necessary, and is not effective against the Deer tick, which may carry Lyme disease. However, a pyrethrum spray is considered the most effective repellent for the Deer tick. You may want to use your dog flea and tick spray on your boot tops and pant cuffs. Lip protection and medications, such as poison ivy or poison oak lotion are also a good idea.

Now that you're ready for any possibility, you need to consider what your Dachshund will need at a Field Trial? Remarkably little: a well fitting collar (you may see Dachshunds at trials wearing an O-ring or safety collar) with one or two tags, a leash to take your Dachshund into and out of the field, a release line (a length of rope about eight feet long) that is passed through the O-ring, D-ring, or collar (the two ends of the line are held in your hands, and when the dog is released to track the rabbit, you drop one end of the rope, and the dog smoothly moves away from the rope).

Your Dachshund will need water in the field. Some of the things that you may see, include leather water bags (botas), hiking water belts, bicycle bottles, and reusable plastic juice bottles. Your Dachshund obviously does not need a rain coat, boots, or a sweater in the field, but in the rain, a mini might be more comfortable if she is wrapped in a towel and carried inside

David Kawami pointing the way.

your rain coat. You will also want towels in your dog gear, for wet days. When in areas where there may be Deer ticks, you should also have a flea and tick spray with a pyrethrum base. I would also suggest a flea comb.

Now that you understand a little more about Field Trials, you are probably asking yourself what the benefit of involvement is. What good is it? What are Field Trial people about, and how are they different from the show (conformation) people?

The simplest answer to the first two questions is that participation is fun for both you and your Dachshund. Remember, the Dachshund is a hunting dog. It was created to hunt both above and below the ground. Like the standard Dachshund, the miniature is also a serious hunting dog, and not a toy version of the breed. The miniature was bred down (created) to meet a specific hunting need. A conscious effort was made to breed a Dachshund that was smaller and had keen hunting instincts. The Dachshund standard and miniature were not bred to simply fit on your lap. While the degree of hunting drive can vary from Dachshund to Dachshund, it is still a hunting dog.

Involvement in the Dachshund Club of America Region VI Rescue program provides the opportunity to see a number of dogs from a wide

In pursuit of the critter.

variety of situations. Most of the Dachshunds rescued are pet shop specials from puppy mills in the Midwest. On rare occasions, one of these rescue dogs will be turned in with AKC papers, and the new owner will want to do something with the dog. With AKC registry papers, the Dachshund can enter Field Trial competition. Recently, one was entered in the Open All Age Dog Class. It was the Dachshund's and the owner's first Field Trial. Amazingly the dog earned a first place. The significance of this is that the instinct to hunt is so basic that even the worst breeding "program" can not breed the need and desire to hunt out of the Dachshund. The Field Trial Dachshund has also been fortunate with regards to the importing of dogs from Germany. While this is not as common as it was in the 1950s, it still happens, allowing new hunting vigor to enter the gene pool.

The first time you see your Dachshund do what it was bred to do (when you see the hunting instincts click in and glimpse the potential that was waiting to be developed), an emotional reaction occurs—one which has the potential to amaze you and your view of the natural world. The simplicity of nature may not seem quite so simple. Field Trialing your Dachshunds, therefore, can possibly change the way you view the natural world.

Canoeing on the Sebasticook River in Maine. *Photo: Kawami.*

In *The New Dachshund* by Lois Meistrell, one can find references to working (hunting) Dachshunds being physically different from show (conformation) dogs. Meistrell states, "None of them would have placed in a breed class, but they were shown with pride . . ." Unfortunately, this sentiment still exists, and the brunt of the criticism is directed at working Wirehair Dachshunds imported from Europe (specifically Germany and France)—I've even heard them referred to as "those ugly dogs." Of course this must be taken with a grain of salt since "those ugly dogs" are often taking home all of the ribbons from the Field Trials. As to not taking a place in a breed conformation class, the first AKC Dual Champion Dachshund (Conformation Champion and Field Trial Champion) was a hunting wirehair from European stock Uta von Moosbach, bred by avid hunter, field trialer, and one of the founders of Deer Search, Dr. John Jeanneney. (See page 134 for Dr. Jeanneney's article)

Having said a prejudice exists, it can also be reported that the prejudice is losing ground. In areas where field trialing is active, Dachshund Specialty Shows now include a Field Trial Class. The Dachshund Club of American National Specialty Show now includes a Field Trial Class, and in 1993, Gatsby, a Dachshund from the Field Trial Class, went on to receive an award of merit in conformation. The Badger Dachshund Club has in addition to a Field Trial Class, a Dual Champion Class at their specialty. In 1995, the centennial for The Dachshund Club of America, a Dual Champion Class was also added. Perhaps more important are the new field trialers who come from the conformation ring. These are serious conformation breeders who view field trialing as fun and necessary to maintain the Dachshund as a hunting dog.

It is hard to imagine what field trialing was like in the 1970s with only three Dachshund Field Trials a year. Currently there are 14 clubs that hold licensed field trials. The field trial season begins the last weekend of September at the Central Ohio Dachshund Club, and DCA Region IV Field Trials held in Chillicothe on the grounds of the Southern Ohio Beagle Club. These are attended by many field trialers from the East Coast as well as those from the Midwest. Guided by Pat Nance, the trials have always been well respected and a joy to run dogs at. The members of the Southern Ohio Beagle Club have always gone out of their way to make sure the Dachshund field trialers have a good time and successful trial. Saturday night after the trial, there is a steak barbecue. What could be better than another trial the next day?

The season then goes into high gear with six field trials in the Midwest, and six on the East Coast. By mid-November, the trial season ends as winter arrives. Those determined to get in more trials can make their way to Davis, CA, where the season is just beginning. Golden Gate Dachshund Club and Northern California Dachshund Club host two trials each. In New York State, as the field trial season ends, the hunting season begins. Members of the Hudson Valley Dachshund Association put on their Deer Search jackets, and wait for calls to assist hunters recover wounded game.

February and March bring four more trials in Davis, California, again hosted by the Golden Gate and Northern California Dachshund Clubs. April takes Californians north to the Greater Portland Dachshund Club field trials. The hardy Northwestern trial through thick brush, inch long thorns, and an occasional brush with poison oak, is held on Oregon State game lands at Monmouth. The Greater Portland Dachshund Club also holds two trials in August. Meanwhile, in the Midwest, there are 7 trials, and on the East Coast there are 6. New York City and Long Island Dachshunds look forward to the Dachshund Association of Long Island and Hudson Valley Dachshund Association field trials on the running grounds of the Long Island Beagle Club in Calverton. These trials are unusual in that a complaint is often heard that there are too many rabbits.

The latest club to field trial is the Bay Colony Dachshund Club (first licensed trial in November 1994), which holds two trials a year: One in the fall with the Connecticut Yankee Dachshund Club (the second club to hold trials), and in the spring with the Albany Capitol Districts Dachshund Club (the third club to hold trials). The season ends in the East with the Dachshund Club of New Jersey's field trial in June, which is held on the grounds of the Central New Jersey Beagle Club in Sergeantsville.

Ch. Ivic's Clever Excuse, CDX, CG "Stripe" gazes across the lake on a misty morning looking for a big one. *Photo: Larsen.*

In the Midwest trials begin in March or early April with one of the pioneers of field trialing in the region, the Midwest Dachshund Club in Michigan. The next is held by the St. Louis Dachshund Club, which began field trialing by hosting the National Field Trial in 1990. The charming Diane Tiller was not only instrumental in starting the St. Louis field program, but assisted another newcomer, the Hoosier Dachshund Club (Indiana), develop their own program. Hoosier (first licensed trial in 1993) hosts two trials in May. The Midwest season ends with the Badger Dachshund Club hosted trials. Badger is one of the most active field trialing clubs in the nation. Possessed by the need to field trial, they crisscross the Midwest in Spring and Fall to attend, and its members are known by the wear on their tires and their gas and motel bills.

With the end of the season, many still find the urge to work their Dachshunds, and fortunately the season's end coincides the time when the farms, orchards, nurseries, and stud farms need assistance in removing Woodchucks. Highlights of the field trial year are The Dachshund Club of America's Annual Field Trial and their National Field Trial. The annual trial is held at the Central New Jersey Beagle Club. This commemorates the first Dachshund Field Trial, held in 1935. It's name is derived from the fact that for a while, it was the year's only field trial. The Annual Field Trial is held in conjunction with the Fall Dachshund Club of New Jersey trial.

The National Field Trial began in 1985, created at the suggestion of avid trialer Don Hickman. The trial attempts to travel through the six regions in conjunction with The Dachshund Club of America's National Specialty (conformation) show.

TYPICAL NATIONAL FIELD TRIAL SCHEDULE

Date	Organization	Location	Event
Aug.	Greater Portland Dachshund Club	Oregon	DCA Region I, Field Trial
Sept.	Central Ohio Dachshund Club	Ohio	DCA Region IV, Field Trial
Oct.	Badger Dachshund Club	Wisconsin	DCA Region IV, Field Trial
	Bay Colony Dachshund Club	Massachusetts	DCA Region IV, Field Trial
	Connecticut Yankee Dachshund Club	Connecticut	DCA Region IV, Field Trial

Date	Organization	Location	Event
	Hoosier Dachshund Club	Indiana	DCA Region IV, Field Trial
	Dachshund Club of New Jersey	New Jersey	DCA Region IV, Field Trial
	Dachshund Club of America "The Annual"	Various	
Nov.	St. Louis Dachshund Club	Missouri	DCA Region IV , Field Trial
	Hudson Valley Dachshund Association	Massachusetts	DCA Region VI, Field Trial
	Northern California Dachshund Club	California	DCA Region I, Field Trial
Dec.	Golden Gate Dachshund Club	California	DCA Region I, Field Trial
Feb.	Golden Gate Dachshund Club	California	DCA Region I, Field Trial
Mar.	Northern California Dachshund Club	California	DCA Region I, Field Trial
Apr.	Midwest Dachshund Club	Michigan	DCA Region VI, Field Trial, (two days)
	Dachshund Association of Long Island	New York	DCA Region IV, Field Trial
	Hudson Valley Dachshund Association	New York	DCA Region IV, Field Trial
	Dachshund Club of St. Louis	Missouri	DCA Region IV, Field Trial

continues

TYPICAL NATIONAL FIELD TRIAL SCHEDULE (CONT.)

Date	Organization	Location	Event
	Bay Colony Dachshund Club	Massachusetts	DCA Region IV, Field Trial
	Albany Capitol District Dachshund Club	New York	DCA Region IV, Field Trial
May	Hoosier Dachshund Club	Indiana	DCA Region IV, Field Trial
Jun.	Dachshund Club of New Jersey	New Jersey	DCA Region IV, Field Trial

The National Field Trial, when held in the Midwest or East is usually held in May or June. When in the West, it is held in February or March.

GOING TO GROUND, THE DEN TRIAL

Here Carrie Hamilton leads us underground through the dark tunnels of The Den Trial:

Den trials for Dachshunds have existed in Europe for over a century. The artificial Dens used for these trials can be quite complex, and many include upward and downward slopes, side tunnels, and internal obstacles, such as sand, water, narrower sections of tunnel, etc. They are therefore often set up at formal, permanent testing sites. Most European den trials allow full or partial contact between the dog and the quarry. Usually a fox or badger is used as the quarry. With animal rights concerns receiving increased attention, the number of trials held each year has declined considerably, and some countries no longer hold such tests.

In 1933, the United States Dachshund Field Trial Club (USDFTC) was established to keep alive the hardy courage and keen hunting instincts of the Dachshund breed by encouraging and holding field (den) trials. However, the effort required to set up the complex underground dens, both for training the dogs and for the actual trials, strained the club's small membership, and interest in the underground tests waned. The USDFTC folded in 1935. Recognizing that, at the very least, a minority of Dachshund enthusiasts felt the goals of the USDFTC were laudable, the Dachshund Club of America (DCA) stepped in. Once difficulties associated with the holding of underground tests led to the demise of the USDFTC, DCA looked for a simpler and more viable alternative test. Thus, in 1935, DCA held the first

AKC approved Dachshund field trial, which was modeled after Beagle brace trials. These above ground field trials were easier to train for and to hold. The above ground trialing format was a success, and Dachshund field trialing is presently a very popular sport.

More recently, an interest in testing the instincts of all "earth" dogs has emerged in the United States. The American Working Terrier Association (AWTA) was formed in 1971 to promote the traditional use of terriers and Dachshunds for earth work and above ground hunting. Through literature and field or den trials, the AWTA hoped to promote the hunting and ownership of terriers and Dachshunds of size, conformation, and character, to perform as working terriers. The AWTA also hoped to encourage breeders to retain the hunting instincts that make these breeds so characteristically "terrier." Without the opportunity to test these instincts, terriers and Dachshunds would cease to be the working dogs that they were meant to be.

The AWTA developed a simpler and safer (for both participants) type of den trial. The AWTA den trial uses caged laboratory rats as the quarry, and a simple and portable tunnel design. The AWTA considers its test to be an instinct test, for which training is not required. There are two levels of testing. They are novice and open. Both use a 9-inch high by 9-inch wide tunnel. The tunnel is formed by digging a trench and placing within it a three-sided wooden den liner. The den liner forms the top and sides of the tunnel, and is covered with dirt so that it is flush with the surface of the ground. The end of the den liner farthest from the tunnel entrance has metal bars across it to prevent the dogs from reaching the caged rats.

The Novice tunnel is ten feet long, and contains one right angle (90 degree) turn. The Novice Class prepares dogs for entering the Open class. The Open tunnel is thirty feet long, and contains three 90 degree turns. A dog is released ten feet from the den, and many reach the quarry within 30 seconds. After reaching the quarry, the dog must "work" (bark, growl, dig, etc.) to indicate her interest in the rats. If the dog works for one full minute, it passes. Dogs qualifying at trials in the Open division receive an AWTA Certificate of Gameness (CG).

Because of the popularity of the AWTA trials, the American Kennel Club has put together its own testing program for earth dogs. The AKC Earthdog Test program has three levels (Junior, Senior, and Master) plus an Introduction to Quarry. The Introduction to Quarry, and Junior level are the same as the AWTA Novice and Open tests, respectively. The only difference is that to earn a Junior Earthdog title (JE), a dog must pass the test twice, each time under a different judge.

Dogs may require some training to pass the Senior and Master levels of the Earthdog test program. The senior test adds a scented, dead-end side tunnel that contains bedding material, and a false unscented exit to the den design used in the junior test. The entrance to the senior den will also be steeper than that used in the Junior test, and the release point will be twenty feet from the den entrance. Besides reaching the quarry in 90 seconds and working for 90 seconds, dogs entered in the Senior test must leave the den on command. After the first two parts of the test are completed, the rats will be removed, and the handler has 90 seconds to call her dog out of the den. A dog must pass the senior level three times under two different judges to earn a Senior Earthdog title (SE).

The Master test adds two internal obstructions to the den design used in the Senior test. One obstruction is a 6 inch diameter piece of PVC pipe that must be climbed over. The height of the tunnel will be raised by 6 inches over the PVC pipe so that the clearance throughout the tunnel remains the same. The other obstruction is a narrowing of the tunnel to a width of 6 inches for a distance of 18 inches. Along with underground work, the Master level will test a dog's ability to work with another dog above ground. Dogs will be braced and released from a point roughly 100 feet from the den entrance. The dogs will be evaluated on their ability to locate the den. Once the den is located, each dog will be tested separately below ground. A dog must pass the Master level four times under two different judges to earn a Master Earthdog title (ME).

For further information on Den Trials, we suggest you contact the AKC.

DACHSHUNDS IN DEER SEARCH

Now that we have seen what Dachshunds can do in a somewhat controlled environment both above and below ground, Dr. John Jeanneney, who will explain how the natural hunting instincts of the Dachshund are put to work, purchased his first Dachshund in 1965, and attended his first field trial a year later. He is experienced in most types of Dachshund field work, but finds the handler-dog partnership of blood tracking to be the most rewarding.

Dr. Jeanneney's article originally appeared in 1994; consequently, some of the statistical information may not be current.

Out of a concern to reduce the wounding and loss of deer during hunting seasons, I began using a Dachshund, Fld.Ch. Clary von Moosbach, to track wounded deer in 1975. Ordinarily this would have been illegal in New York, but the experiment was authorized by the State Department of Environmental Conservation (DEC). At this point I had already owned and hunted

A well-earned dip follows a day underground.

wires for nine years, had read about the tasks of working Dachshunds in Europe, and had received some training from Hubert Stoquert, a breeder and handler who was regional wildlife manager for the part of France adjacent to the German frontier. Blood tracking, I learned, was a term usually applied to an activity where there was no visible blood to track, and the dog often used other sources of scent to find the wounded big game.

The Deer Search organization originated with a small group of people in Dutchess County, New York, who worked together in the early research phase. Hans Klein, Don Hickman, and Sid Baker all began working with Wirehaired Dachshunds which were small, attractive, capable of doing the job, and conveniently available. At first, Deer Search operated as an experimental program testing the practical feasibility and public acceptance of what was originally considered in this country to be a highly controversial practice. Deer Search was also very active in hunter education to reduce the number of deer that were wounded in the first place.

In 1986, after years of public education and lobbying, a New York Conservation law amendment was passed providing for the licensed use of leashed tracking dogs to find wounded deer and bear. It was not until 1989 that the final details of implementation were worked out in the form of DEC

The late Don Hickman with his renowned tracking dog, field Ch. Adelheide Von Spurlaut.

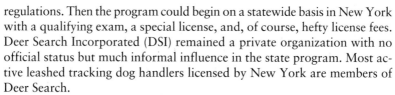

regulations. Then the program could begin on a statewide basis in New York with a qualifying exam, a special license, and, of course, hefty license fees. Deer Search Incorporated (DSI) remained a private organization with no official status but much informal influence in the state program. Most active leashed tracking dog handlers licensed by New York are members of Deer Search.

The inspiration for Deer Search came originally from Germany, but it was necessary to adapt European practice to the American circumstances of the Northeast. Tracking dogs are worked at all times on a long leash and never released on wounded game. Conservation officers and other police officers are informed prior to every call. Recognizing the frontier individualism and do-it-yourself tradition of American hunting, we advise hunters to do everything they can to find their own deer, and to call us only as a last resort.

Today Deer Search has expanded to over 100 members divided into eastern and western New York chapters. In addition, there are pilot programs run by Deer Search members in Vermont and Wisconsin. Since 1975, almost 800 wounded deer have been found for hunters by Deer Search handlers. In all but a handful of cases, these deer were and are being found by Dachshunds. This is not at all what I originally expected. Dachshunds were never taken seriously by most American hunters, and it seemed that German Shorthaired and Wirehaired pointers would probably take over in Deer Search. The original continental versions of these breeds had long ago proved themselves in Europe, and Americanized versions were widespread and respected here. A promising blood tracking program in Indiana based upon German Wirehaired pointers had been started slightly before the Deer Search experiment, and had then collapsed for reasons that were largely political. The Dachshund did prevail in Deer Search despite the fact that the organization has never officially or unofficially advocated using a particular breed of dog.

Almost all of the dogs used in Deer Search have been wires of recent European ancestry, but one of the very best was a thirteen pound wire with only a slight dash of German Zwergteckel blood in his veins. Fld.Ch. Nikki XXI excelled because of nose, intelligence, and sheer strength of character. In Europe, longs and smooths do blood tracking work, but we have had no experience with them in Deer Search.

Currently, our most effective alternate to the Dachshund has been a basset, another short-legged dog, which is being used in a pilot research program by DSI member, Tim Nichols in Vermont. A number of DSI handlers who had owned or specialized in larger breeds have come around to the position that under most conditions encountered in the Northeast, an intelligent, agile Dachshund is easier to work with.

To more clearly illustrate the problems faced by handlers and dogs in blood tracking work, it is useful to consider several common tracking situations which arise again and again. Let's examine two hypothetical "deer calls." The first call illustrates psychological challenges that are faced many times each season by a busy tracking dog. A bowhunter calls just after dark, after searching all day for a deer that he shot at dawn. Just as he released the arrow, the deer took a step forward and the broadhead penetrated too far back. Over the phone the hunter explains that there are splatters of blood for 200 yards, but beyond this point no trace is visible to follow. After informing the local DEC conservation officer and the State Police concerning details about the hunter, location of the site and landowner permission, you go to the area and meet the hunter.

You usually begin by asking your dog to track again over the visible blood line originally followed by the hunter. This acquaints the dog with the particular scent you wish him to follow. After you pass the hunter's point of loss you and your dog are on your own. Did the deer simply stop bleeding, or did he backtrack for a distance over the original line? The point of loss area is tracked up and muddled where the hunter walked back and forth searching and inadvertently spreading the wounded deer's scent in ways that the deer did not go. Getting started here is the hardest part, and here, like a guide dog leading the blind, the leashed tracking dog must take responsibility, and the handler must have confidence in his canine partner. There may be false starts in wrong directions; the dog must correct himself if necessary, and the handler must "read" the dog and assess his degree of certainty.

Once the right direction of the line away from the point of loss has been established, the problems are not over. After dark other deer in the area strolled repeatedly across the 12-hour old scent line of the wounded deer leaving "hot lines" much fresher and more enticing. The leashed tracking dog will typically go a half mile or more in these conditions, without visible blood to confirm the line, before the wounded or already dead deer is found.

These situations are real challenges, and to succeed takes more than just a good nose and a burning desire to pursue game. The dog must be both wise and committed to pleasing his handler by nosing out and following the correct scent line. The tendency of Dachshunds to relate to an individual master, rather than to a pack, gives them an edge over many other breeds of scent hounds, some of which may have even finer noses, but are indifferent to their handler, and ready to follow the hottest scent encountered. Over the years I have become convinced that a fine balance of discriminating initiative and "biddableness" is of more practical value than olfactory power alone.

The Dachshunds and the specialized Bloodhounds (Hanover bloodhounds and Bavarian mountain bloodhounds) all seem to yield more biddable, handler-oriented individuals than most other breeds of scent hounds. The continental pointing breeds, developed to work in close cooperation with the hunter, have a similar psychological profile in this respect. It is probably the physical characteristics of Dachshunds, particularly the wires, that make them appear at present to be the most practical breed for the field conditions encountered in the Northeast.

A second deer call scenario, which includes typical challenges of vegetation and terrain, illustrates qualities of different physical types of tracking dogs. In this hypothetical composite case, a Deer Search handler and dog have been called in to track a large buck that has been wounded in the

More suited to going under obstacles, Dachshunds will still climb in pursuit of game. *Photo: Kawami.*

shoulder. The buck is likely to go a long way and may still be alive when found.

When such a case occurs in Germany, one of the larger blood tracking breeds weighing 70 pounds or more is likely to be called. These dogs, with their great strength and speed, are worked off lead; they have pull-down power if it is needed. But in most parts of the United States this counts for little, since releasing a dog on wounded game is both unacceptable and illegal.

Tracking the wounded big buck we find that he has passed into dense thickets of briars and multiflora rose. A Dachshund, standard size or smaller, can pass under the thorns while the handler, clad in heavy Cordura nylon presses through gingerly or even crawls underneath on hands and knees. This kind of exercise is not much fun with a driving, pointer-sized dog unless that dog has an exquisite understanding of the word "whoa."

Sometimes the buck charges on into a big swamp with water over the handler's knees. Here the long legged dog has the edge; he is tall enough to follow what little deer scent has been left on swamp vegetation. A good standard Dachshund can swim from bog to bog, following almost as well although his nose cannot reach as high. If the water is near the freezing point a standard wire with a really good double coat can still work long and effectively. Standard longs, smooths, and particularly minis with their smaller body mass would theoretically be more susceptible to heat loss. However we have seen near minis with poor wire coats do amazingly well. Up to a point, sheer will can overcome physical disadvantage.

Out of the swamps and back on high ground, the handler and dog track cross the abandoned fields now so common in the Northeast. Burdocks and Sticktights are everywhere. A correctly coated wire does not load up with them, nor would a smooth. My own poorly-coated wire has been stopped cold on a few occasions when his eyes and whole head were obscured by a helmet of burrs or sticktights that took an hour to remove. Longs, in the same circumstances, would certainly suffer equal inconvenience.

Now the buck is up from his bed and keeping well out ahead of handler and dog. In the overgrown fields the tracking dog is constantly having to force his way through heavy vegetation; the constant friction of the tracking leash also drains energy. For the strong standard Dachshund or a dog even larger, all this is much easier than for the dog under fifteen pounds. Sound, sensible conformation contributes to drive and stamina; real blood tracking reminds us that decent ground clearance is part of sensible conformation and essential to the working Dachshund. A tough deer call is much more taxing to a Dachshund than a field trial. If a busy tracking dog is too low in the chest it will be covered with bruises, sores and scabs before the season is half over.

The buck makes its last stand in a woodlot crisscrossed with fallen branches and tree trunks. For the tiring Dachshund, length of leg sufficient for jumping over logs is again invaluable. When the buck drops at the final merciful shot, the search and chase are over. For both dog and handler, desire and perseverance have prevailed. Out of such blood tracking experiences comes an awareness that the physical Dachshund is well-suited for the task of finding wounded big game as it is being done in America. But the essence of the blood tracking Dachshund goes beyond what is seen with the eyes and felt with the fingers. Most important are responsiveness to the handler, discriminating intelligence and indomitable will. Experience pulls it all together; as blood trackers, Dachshunds do not reach their peak until eight or ten.

DACHSHUNDS AS THERAPY DOGS

When Veterinarian Dr. Kit Walker heard we were writing a book on Dachshunds, she sent us a charming letter and an essay on the use of Dachshunds as therapy dogs. We were so touched that we knew the book would not be complete without its inclusion, and have therefore reprinted both her letter and essay.

Dear Dee,

Please find enclosed the write-up about Dachshunds involved in therapy dog work. Thank you for the opportunity to have this topic included; it has been near and dear to me for a number of years now. The dog in the enclosed photos is Harriet, my mini that passed away this July. Besides eating and playing with endless tennis balls, her true forte was as a therapy dog. I believe that when her harness went on for a visit, she knew exactly what was expected of her. She was always a little lady, always on her best behavior, and so very willing and able to please anyone she met. When she died, I realized through the many cards and letters I received just how many people knew and were touched by this amazing little dog.

Perhaps others who may read the book will be encouraged to try therapy work with their doxie, and know the joy of the bond established between handler and pet just as I did with Harriet.

It was a pleasure to meet you. Thank you for allowing me to ramble a bit.

Most sincerely,
Kit Walter

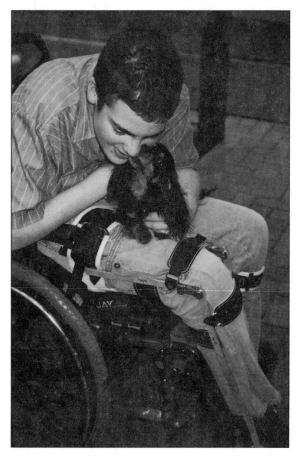

"Harriet" and friend.

The use of dogs (and other species) as adjunct therapy in many human conditions/disorders has been widely documented in recent years. The benefits provided by these animals are as numerous as the situations they enter. Whether the dog visits a nursing home to cheer this often immobile group of people, or helps a mentally or physically challenged individual to focus elsewhere for a brief time, it appears that the success of pet therapy boils down to the unconditional love and sense of need that pets give us.

Therapy dog work seems like a rather natural occupation for the exuberant Dachshund. They are willing to please almost to a fault. With tail a-wagging and tongue a-licking, the Dachshund is invariably a crowd-pleaser. As a breed, they are recognizable, sometimes creating a link to a happy memory of an existing or former pet; they are portable and non-threatening, usually making themselves comfortable on a bed, or in someone's arms. Surely if form follows function, the Dachshund was designed not only for the den, but also for the lap.

Even though there are uncountable stories associated with therapy dog visits, perhaps the inclusion of two or three at this point would help to illustrate the profound effect that these dogs often have on the people whose lives they touch.

A severely injured young man waking from a coma of several weeks is delighted that Harriet, a mini longhair (see picture), loves to sit in his lap and give kisses in spite of his braces, tracheotomy, and other supportive equipment. She is unaffected by his appearance. Over the next few months, the dog becomes his incentive to try to establish enough movement in an injured arm to hold and pet her. This patient would later relate to Harriet's owner/handler that the dog was his first memory after the coma, and that her name was the first word he spoke when his speech returned.

An older nursing home resident is so taken with a visiting therapy dog that he requests in his will that the dog be present at his wake and graveside service; a request that ultimately came to pass.

Another older resident at a Veteran's home will not play the piano for staff or other residents, but will play with gusto for the visiting therapy dog who accompanies him with harmonious howling.

It is very often the case that the staff members at visitation sites also reap the benefits of the visiting dogs, and actively seek out a cold nose and a warm kiss.

Getting your Dachshund involved in an active therapy program may be as easy as contacting a local obedience or breed club. There are a number of national organizations through which a dog may become registered. When all is said and done, the level of success of any visit is measured by the smiles of the recipients, the wag of the dog, and the warmth in your heart.

DACHSHUND RACING

Thanks to Dr. Jeanneney and others who have made invaluable contributions to this book out of their love for the breed, we are realizing that the Dachshund is a much more versatile dog than one would have initially imagined. The story would not be complete, however, without a discussion of Dachshund racing.

Recently, Dachshund racing has been given national attention in both televised and printed media. From watching and reading, one would have the impression that this is a totally new phenomenon. In fact, Dachshund "racing," though it has evolved from its original form, has been around for over 30 years.

In the early 1960's the Eastern Coursing Club, founded by Bob and Babby Tongren of Afghan fame, began holding coursing (racing) events for Afghan Hounds and Salukis on the property of successful and longtime breeders of Dachshunds George and Dottie Pickett in Sherman, Connecticut. Their land was ideally suited for lure coursing.

The Afghans were placed in starting boxes, and permitted to see and smell a rabbit skin lure that was attached to a long line, which ran from the starting line to the finish, where it was attached to a manually turned reel. The dogs were released from their starting boxes at the same time the lure was being retracted onto the reel. They would chase the lure to the finish, and the first to cross was the winner. It just so happened, that the starting line co-incided with a large paddock area filled with Dottie's Dachshunds. It didn't take long to notice that the Dachshunds were not only enthusiastic observers, but wanted to be willing participants. In short, they went nuts.

One afternoon, Bob Tongren who was also an avid Dachshund fan, decided to see what the short-legged ones would do on the race course. Obviously, the track had to be shortened. While we are not sure of the exact dimensions (if there were any), the course was approximately 100 feet long and 50 feet wide, with a start and finish line, and fenced along its entire length to keep the dogs within the confines of the track.

The Dachshunds were placed in the starting boxes, shown the lure, and released. To the delight of both Dachshunds and owners, the race was over almost as fast as it began. The dogs loved the boxes, and once released, never looked back. Dachshund racing was born.

It didn't take long for the word to spread, and weekends would bring increasing numbers of Dachshund breeders and owners from every direction just to watch their Dachshunds race. There was a fun, informal atmosphere with children, blankets, and picnic baskets the norm. There were no entry fees, and no prizes were awarded. It was a fun day in the sun, where people would enjoy the races, and talk Dachshunds. Both Peggy Westphal's and our children would race to the finish line to retrieve the lure. The one who returned it to the starting line received a nickel, so the old folks wouldn't tire.

In June of 1966, Dachshund racing made its debut to the public at the Greenwich (Connecticut) Kennel Club Annual Conformation Show (then under the able leadership of the famous and respected Dachshund breeder and judge, Jeannette W. Cross). It was so enthusiastically accepted by the spectators that it remained a permanent fixture for the next several years.

It wasn't long before the fun sport of Dachshund racing found its way to the west coast, and in 1968 the Golden Gate Kennel Club hosted the first public racing of Dachshunds at their dog show in the Cow Palace. And in November of 1974, the Cascade Dachshund Club of Washington held its first exhibition at the Whitbey Island Kennel Club Show. These were all fun races, and for many years, both Dachshunds and spectators alike enjoyed chasing and watching that lure—just out of the dog's reach—bouncing down the 100 foot course.

At the Dachshund Club of America shows, we had what we called fun night, held sometime during the middle of the week. This was a time for Dachshunds and exhibitors alike to let down their hair, relax, and relieve some of the tension of the shows. Racing would go on until the wee hours of the morning.

Sadly, in 1995, Dachshund racing began turning up in TV Ads, and on televised Greyhound track racing. The fun had left the sport. Money became

A well-earned lazy day on the river. *Photo: Larsen.*

the motivating factor as large crowds began turning out to watch our short-legged friends race at Greyhound racing events. Greyhound mutual tracks had been losing their appeal for many years, and something was needed to bring back the crowds. Dachshund racing seemed to be the answer, and while no betting was permitted, profits from the Greyhound races began to increase. Caring Dachshund people began to realize that betting was not far behind, ultimately resulting in indiscriminate breeding for profit. The Dachshund was about to suffer the same cruel fate as the Greyhound.

Out of necessity, the Board of Directors of the Dachshund Club of America took the position that Dachshunds were not bred to race, and what was once done for fun had gone too far. Members were asked not to race Dachshunds under any circumstances (including for fun).

It was also requested that we do everything legally and morally possible to discourage and stop organized Dachshund racing at tracks and refuse to breed or to sell puppies knowingly to anyone interested in engaging in this practice.

With the help of all Dachshund lovers, we can perhaps, in a few years time, return to our fun nights at DCA and our Sunday afternoons in the sun, letting our short-legged little ones enjoy chasing the lure.

chapter 12

The History of the Dachshund

Our intention here is not to document the many successful show dogs and the people responsible for making the breed so popular today. Such an attempt always runs the risk of leaving out both great dogs and great people who have contributed so much to the breed's evolution during the modern era. Neither will we relate the known early days of Dachshunds in Germany and England, already documented extensively in other publications. Rather, we will concentrate on the Dachshund's origins—both fact and speculation.

History, by definition, is an account of a known past based on recorded fact. As such, it may only be refuted or enhanced by the discovery of previously unknown information. *Theories* and *speculations* have not as yet been proven (though both are *based* in fact), and must therefore be regarded only as informed opinion. Unfortunately, the Dachshund's history falls into the latter two categories, with much controversy surrounding its origins.

We have related to you our lifetime of experiences with Dachshunds— we know, understand, and love them, but we know little about their origins. Significant research has been conducted by Jeannette W. Cross, Lois Meistrell (as published in her book *The New Dachshund,* 1976), and the late John Hutchinson Cook on the Dachshund's history.

We present you with an informed anthology of writers and research both past and present to help sort out the various facts and theories surrounding this breed.

While it is not known precisely where or when the Dachshund as we know it appeared on the scene, the general consensus is that it emerged out of either Austria or Germany sometime between the seventeenth and eighteenth centuries. Some, however, believe that the Dachshund's origins can be traced back to centuries before the birth of Christ.

Illustrations from *The Complete German Hunter* by Flemming, 1719.

ST. HUBERT, THE BASSET HOUND, AND THE DACHSHUND

On the breed's history, Lois Meistrell writes the following:

A sinner turned saint, a poor Emperor who wed a Duke's daughter, the hunting habits of the Pharaohs, and a theory that Dachshunds may not be of German origin after all, are among the tales told of the breed's history. Sorted out from these legends and ancient tales are facts that warrant serious consideration as to how the Dachshund came into being.

There is more fancy than fact in many of these stories, but real or imagined, they make interesting reading. Actually, no one really knows the origin of the Dachshund, or for that matter the origin of a large number of breeds as we know them today. It remains that Dachshunds did arrive, and judging from current registration figures they are here to stay.

Dachs 16, in the first Dachshund studbook, and Figure, the first and founding sire of the Morgan breed of horse, have in common that their ancestries have never been proven, and their offspring have been a reproduction of their own images for centuries.

All dogs, Dachshunds included, are descended from a small, prehistoric animal, the Tomarctus, that lived on the earth fifteen million years ago. The only present day animal that resembles it in any way is the civet cat, a mammal that lives in the warmer regions of the Old World and has been described as a weasel-cat, since it displays the characteristics of both. From the Tomarctus came four distinct varieties of the Canis Familiaris and it is from the Canis Familiaris Leinere that the hound family (of which the Dachshund is a member) is descended.

Archaeological evidence points to the Saluki, the Afghan, the Greyhound and possibly the Borzoi as being the oldest of the hound breeds. These dogs were the ancestors of the Sleuth hound, a large, early version of the Bloodhound, which in time, was the progenitor of the St. Hubert hound, a breed of fine scenting and hunting ability that was bred by the monks of the monastery of St. Hubert in the Ardennes section of Belgium. It is from the St. Hubert hound that authorities believe that the Basset Hound, the Beagle, and the Dachshund are descended. The St. Hubert hound also had a strong influence on many other hound breeds.

These hounds derive their name from the patron saint of hounds and hunting, St. Hubert, who lived from 656 to 727 A.D. A Duke's son, as a young man he had led a completely dissolute life. One Good Friday, the cynical, irreverent young fellow—at the peak of his wayward ways—scoffed at worship on the holy day and took to the forest with his horse and hounds to hunt. Luck was with him, for he had not penetrated the woodlands very far when he sighted a magnificent stag. Raising his bow to take aim, he got the fright of his life when, between the stag's antlers, there appeared a cross. (To this day, the stag with a cross between its antlers is the emblem of St. Hubert.) Hubert left the forest and went straight to church, where he confessed his many sins, received absolution and from that time on led a life of such exemplary piety that he became Bishop of Liege. He founded the monastery that bears his name and, some time later, was beatified [sic] by the Roman Catholic Church.

The religious life did not dull his enthusiasm for hunting. From the time of its founding, St. Hubert's monastery maintained a pack of hunting hounds.

The St. Hubert hound is mentioned in the writings of Charles IX (1550-1574) and by Du Fouilloux in his book *La Venerie* (*The Hunt*), written in 1585. The hounds are described as low-set, medium-sized, long in body, not very speedy but possessed of exceptionally accurate scenting powers and pleasingly mellow voices.

Accepting the premise that the Basset Hound and the Dachshund have a common ancestor in the St. Hubert hound, one then wonders how the Basset and the Dachshund became two separate but related breeds, and which was developed first.

The relationship between the Dachshund and the Basset is a highly acceptable concept. Sir John Buchanan-Jardine, in his book *Hounds of the World,* describes four varieties of Bassets known in France. They were the

Artois Basset, the Vendee Basset, the Basset Bleu de Gascogne and the Basset Faune de Bretagne. Of the Basset Bleu, he has this to say, "At first sight, these Gascogne Bassets remind one very strongly of German Dachshunds; the general build is very similar, which, with the rather pointed nose, helps increase the resemblance.

The first edition of *British Dogs* by Hugh Dalziel was published in London in 1897 and quotes a Basset hound fancier who wrote under the pen name "Wildflower." After first explaining that the French and Belgian Bassets are divided into three main classes—Bassets a jambes droites (straight-legged), Bassets a jambes demi-torses (forelegs half crooked), and Bassets a jambes torses (fully crooked)—Wildflower says, ". . . a Black and Tan or a Red Basset a jambes torses cannot by any possible use of one's eyes be distinguished from a Dachshund of the same colour, although some German writers assert that the breeds are quite distinct." E. Fitch Daglish, the English author and Dachshund breeder also supported this concept and used the same quotation in his book, *The Popular Dachshund,* published in London in 1960.

Assuming that the Dachshund and the Basset Hound were once one in the same, which breed emerged first? Probably the Basset, or at least a Basset-like type of short-legged hound. A dog very similar to a Basset could be produced by several generations of selective breeding that utilizes low-stationed individuals from one of the larger hound breeds, such as the Bloodhound (considered to be a leggier replica of the St. Hubert hound).

The Development of the Dachshund

How these short-legged Basset-like descendants of the hounds of St. Hubert developed into Dachshunds is explained by the late John Hutchinson Cook, Dachshund breeder, judge, and a serious student of all hound breeds. He presents a credible theory and one that also raises a question as to whether the Dachshund might have originated in Austria and later migrated to Germany. He expresses the following:

It would appear that a link exists between the history of the Dachshund and that of the imperial Hapsburg family, who ruled Austria until 1918. In 1477, the eighteen-year-old Hapsburg heir, the Holy Roman Emperor Maximillian I, journeyed west from Vienna to Burgundy to become the husband of Marie of Burgundy, daughter and heiress of Charles the Bold, Duke of Burgundy. Maximillian knew he was marrying into a family of great power and wealth, but this knowledge did not prepare him for the awesome magnificence of the Burgundian court. Having grown up in war-torn, impoverished Austria, in his family's cold and barren castle, the young emperor was bedazzled by the opulence and beauty of his father-in-law's palaces. He wrote letters to relatives in Austria describing the wonders of the Burgundian ducal establishment and made particular mention of what impressed him most of all the marvels he found there—Marie's father kept three thousand trained falcons and four thousand trained hunting hounds for his hunting pleasure.

At first thought, four thousand seems an incredible number of hounds for anyone to keep—be he duke, prince, king, or emperor; however, when some of the circumstances are considered, perhaps it really isn't. For one thing, Charles the Bold was richer than most kings, and his lands more extensive. Today, one thinks of Burgundy as a French Province, or perhaps a red wine, but in the fifteenth century, the Duchy of Burgundy embraced the larger part of present-day Belgium, the Netherlands, Luxembourg, and huge areas of northern and northeastern France. Charles could probably have supported twice as many hounds had he chosen to do so.

The second factor was the absolute passion for hunting possessed by the exclusion of just about all other activities. The Austrian nobles who had accompanied Maximillian to Burgundy were apparently favorably impressed with the hounds, for when they returned to Austria, they took some Burgundian hounds home with them. They then placed them in packs and hunted with them. From these hounds, through selective breeding, Mr. Cook theorizes that the Dachshund evolved.

The Dachskrieger, the Huhnerhund, and the Wachtelhund (all now extinct German breeds) have also been credited as being ancestors of the Dachshund. It is quite possible that either the St. Hubert or Burgundian hounds, lost during an extended hunt or given as gifts to German princes, were mated with these native German dogs, producing the Dachshund simultaneously with those that were being bred in Austria.

In the May 1994 issue of *DOGworld*, Dennis Burnside, a freelance writer offers more incite into the early history of the Dachshund:

> The Dachshund was around long before Prussian district forester August von Daacke increased the breed's scenting ability by breeding them with Harzen or Hannoverian Schweisshunds in the early 1800s. The Dachshund (badger dog), also called a Teckel, probably a dialect from Dachel, was developed to hunt deer, boar, fox and, of course, badger. Since the 25- to 40-pound Old World badger, Meles meles, has been around for 65 million years, and certainly during the Neanderthal period, 50,000 to 100,000 years ago, he undoubtedly precedes his canine tormentor.

While we've no Neanderthal Dachshunds, Czech zoologist J.N. Woolwich found some Bronze Age Dachshund-like skeletons near the ashes of burned huts between Silesia (what was northern Czechoslovakia) and the Danube, (not far from the Harz mountains). These "ash" dogs existed 3,000 or 4,000 years ago, and may be the common ancestor of the Pointer, Setter, Spaniel, and Dachshund.

Crooked and straight-legged Dachshunds, according to Georges de Buffon, French naturalist.

Some dog fanciers have hypothesized that the Dachshund originated as an aberration of Nature, that he is achondroplastic. Achondroplasia is a type of dwarfism in which the trunk is of normal size, but the limbs are too short. However, achondroplasia is not hereditary in that one or even both achondroplastic parents may give birth to properly proportioned children.

THE DACHSHUND IN THE VISUAL ARTS

Another way that we can trace historical events is through artistic output. All art is a representation of the world as it was perceived by the artist during the era in which that art was produced. So, when Dachshund-like animals pop up in seventh century artwork, it helps to clue us in with regard to when the breed began to develop.

Brass Rubbings

Some years ago, while visiting the Place des Arts in Montreal, David Blum came across an exhibit of brass rubbings—precise impressions which were painstakingly traced by modern scholars from engraved metal plates found in English churches. He relates the following:

The original metal plates (known as monumental brasses) date mainly from medieval times and often depict the leaders of feudal society. They offer a valuable picture of English life during the period.

One rubbing in particular caught my eye—that of Sir William Fitzralph, whose brass image is found in the church in Pebmarsh, a northeast Essex village of which he was Lord. Curled at Sir William's feet is a dog—a symbol of fidelity—and this dog appears to be a Dachshund. A surprising aspect of this is that the date of the brass monument is 1323—long before Dachshunds were supposed to exist in England. Bruce was able to purchase the brass rubbing. He has also obtained documentation from the Royal Commission on Historic Monuments, which authenticates the date of the original brass engraving.

Coptic Tapestry

Mrs. Jeannette W. Cross is a Dachshund breeder, exhibitor, and judge. She is also an authority on needlework, past and present. She called to our attention a Coptic (fifth or sixth century) wall-hanging of wool-embroidered linen owned by the Metropolitan Museum of Art. The left panel of the hanging shows a horseman accompanied by a dog that Mrs. Cross considers to be a fair likeness of a Basset or Dachshund. Mrs. Cross does not subscribe to the "Egyptian" theory of Dachshund origin, but she did point out that the hanging was the only Egyptian work to show anything that looked remotely like a Dachshund.

I am in complete agreement with Jeannette Cross that the dog represented in The Metropolitan Museum of Art's Coptic textile is a Dachshund ancestor. I would like to add that the Copts inhabited the very locations in present-day Egypt where the Dachshund is represented. In fact, one of the tombs where Dachshunds were depicted was whitewashed by the Copts and one other tomb was turned into a church.

Undoubtedly, ancestors of Dachshunds existed in all of these areas, and therefore, they were represented in Coptic art. After all the word *Copt* is ultimately derived from the Greek word for "Egyptian."

It is because of pieces like this textile that some have come to believe that the breed's origins are actually thousands of years old.

The Dachshund in Antiquity

Judging from the Egyptian paintings, at least some of the first Dachshunds were dappled. The Archduchess Dorothea of Hapsburg expressed that her Imperial family always had gray dappled Dachshunds with blue eyes. So as much as we prize the black and tan, and red dogs today, it appears that at least one Imperial household, dating back to the eleventh century, shared the Egyptian preference for the dappled smooth breed. Royalty does have the tendency to follow traditions established in earlier periods. Perhaps we can hypothesize that Dachshunds were the spoils of conquest or perhaps royal gifts which found their way to Europe.

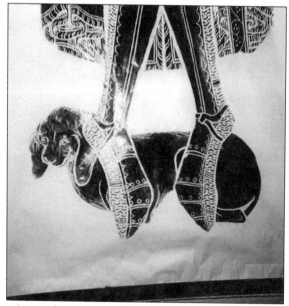

Sir William Fitzralph with dog curled at his feet.

One proponent of the antiquity theory is Major Emil Ilgner, who was elected the first president of the German Dachshund Club in 1888. The theory was widely accepted then and still has many adherents today. Major Ilgner was convinced that a breed's status was enhanced if it could be shown to be of great antiquity. To depict a breed as the most ancient—and therefore the

Detail from a linen and wool wall-hanging (V Century A.D.) depicting an Egyptian horseman with dog, and another hunting lion.

most honorable—seems to have been an obsession for many who wrote on the origins of various breeds. In their writings, one finds such phrases as "comrade of the Vikings," "origin lost in the mists of time," "of considerable antiquity," "of very ancient lineage," and so on. In his book, published in 1896, Ilgner declared that the Dachshund's history could be traced back thirty-five centuries.

Ilgner's conclusions are founded on shaky evidence. Carvings, murals, and inscriptions discovered in ancient Egyptian tombs do show short-legged dogs, but likening them to Dachshunds requires a vivid imagination. The dogs represented are prick-eared and snipy-nosed. Furthermore, drawing conclusions from Egyptian works of art as to the actual size of the object depicted is impossible. Egyptian artists ignored relative proportions altogether. For instance, in a painting showing a pharaoh in the company of other people, the pharaoh figure would be drawn larger than any of the others in order to demonstrate the ruler's importance. Secondly, the work of these artists was so highly stylized that the artistic representations are distorted from the animal's actual appearance.

Much ado has also been made over an inscription on a monument to Thutmose III. The hieroglyphs of the inscription were wrongly translated as "teckal," or "teckar," and the fact that the word "teckel" is synonymous with "Dachshund" in German, the monument was seized upon as evidence of the breed's 4,000-year-old existence. This conclusion was drawn in spite of the fact that the dog shown in connection with the inscription does not bear the slightest resemblance to a Dachshund and looks, in fact, to be more of a Mastiff-type animal.

In a 4,000-year-old Egyptian tomb, what appears to be a Dachshund-type bitch is represented together with a mate of the identical species along with a Greyhound. The three dogs are depicted accompanying their master, Chnemhetep, on a stroll around his domain.

The triad of canines are painted realistically and in scale one to the other and with their patron. The Dachshunds are also similar in size to their modern Standard smooth counterparts.

The Egyptian Dachshund forebears had cropped ears. This was clearly an esthetic feature preferred by their owners. This preference is also evidenced by cropped ears on other breeds such as Salukis, Greyhounds, and Mastiffs.

Smooth Dachshunds may have a royal claim. During the Middle Kingdom, the Dachshund may have been the preferred pet of the Princes of the Nomes of Oryx, Hare, and Elephantine. On bas and sunken reliefs and wall paintings of the various royal tombs of the XII Dynasty (1991–1768 B.C.), the Dachshund-types are represented and placed in the most honored position, directly underneath the princely throne upon which the Royal Master sits, or accompanying the prince on a royal walk or during a royal inspection tour.

Some mention a hieroglyph of a short-legged dog on a monument to Tuthmoses III but neglect to state what kind of monument it is or its location. Tuthmoses III (1504–1450 B.C.) was one of the most powerful pharaohs. He extended Egyptian rule and influence over neighboring countries

The tomb of Chnemhetep.

and built countless monuments up and down the Nile. He often erased the name of a predecessor, replacing it with his own—especially that of his aunt Queen Hatshepsut (1503–1482 B.C.). Even if such a hieroglyph exists, the experts have rejected the hypothesis. Without a more specific location or citation, it is impossible to know if this example is extant.

At three different sites in Egypt, tomb paintings, bas reliefs, and sunken reliefs show what is a very close relative to a smooth Dachshund. If one compares paintings and woodcuts of Dachshunds of the eighteenth and nineteenth centuries (to say nothing of photographs of Dachshunds of the early part of our century with today's beautiful examples), the Egyptian ancestors of four thousand years ago are close indeed.

One might also respectfully take issue with Lois Meistrell's comment that Egyptian artists painted only stylized representations of people and animals. It is true that more important people are often shown larger than the lesser. However, to the contrary, the Egyptians are well known for their elegant and realistic portrayal of animals. Remember, too, that tomb paintings had to be accurate records of the events of a person's life, recount conquests, the founding of cities, treaties, and everyday life such as hunting, fishing, husbandry, dyeing, and weaving. Some feel that these paintings should be considered literal representations, not stylized or presenting abstract concepts.

Around 1900 B.C., during the reign of Pharaoh Sesostris I in Egypt, pictures of short dogs, including one named Ankhu, indicate that the Egyptians enjoyed Dachshund types, some of which were used to hunt badgers, foxes, and other small game which they killed underground.

Professor Iris Cornelia Love, internationally famous archaeologist, and breeder of Dachshunds, offers her personal view of "The Triumphal Procession of Dachshunds Through Time." Her own experiences with Dachshunds, coupled with her archaeological discoveries and unique, first-hand knowledge of ancient Egyptian and Greek civilizations provide an entertaining and educational contribution to the history of the breed. She conveys the following:

> Some 2,275 years ago, some 2,400 hounds walked in a magnificent international procession. This incredible spectacle took place in Egypt in the city of Alexandria.
>
> Athenaeus recounts that "in the procession marched two hunters carrying gilded hunting spears: dogs were also led along numbering 2,400, some Indian, others were Hycarnian or Molossian or of other breeds. Next came one hundred and fifty men carrying trees on which were suspended all sorts of animals and birds."
>
> Among the myriad hounds from distant lands were those from "Crete who were tall and strong" and those from Egypt who were short and long.
>
> The splendor and pleasure that one could derive from witnessing two thousand four hundred hounds marching together (only one hundred less than the entire entry of the great Westminster Kennel Club Show) defies one's imagination, but let us try.

Iris Love and Champion Dachsmith Love's Tyche Tyche. *Photo: Sydney Stafford.*

Picture the majestic and varied assembly of dogs, the finest representatives from kennels culled from every part of Alexander the Great's Empire: from Eastern lands and Western countries; Laconian, Sicilian, Scottish, and Locrian; "some with heavy jowls that fit them for big game—some, swift of foot—some keen of scent; shaggy Cretans bay, slender Spartans and Britons that can break the back of mighty bulls . . . moving in order down painted marble colonnaded Boulevards." This remarkable canine army was dressed in collars of gold and silver which were inlaid with intricate designs and studded with jewels from which bells hung and rung.

Perhaps most importantly, among these exquisite and elegantly subjects, may have been jubilant Smooth Dachshunds. These Egyptian forebears were probably exulting in the knowledge that even then, in 279 or 278 B.C., their ancient and royal ancestry dated back yet another two thousand years.

This spectacular pageant was sponsored and paid for by Ptolemy II, the second Macedonian King to reign over Egypt after the death of Alexander the Great. The procession was called "Pompe Ptolemaios", (*Pompe* in ancient Greek means "procession"). It probably had its origin in religious ceremonies. Some "pompai" were held in honor of newlyweds, others in honor of the dead. Still others, like the "Pompe Ptolemaios" were celebratory, in honor of a particular god or gods. Ptolemy probably orchestrated the ceremony to honor Dionysus, the God of wine, and to celebrate his conquest and triumphal return from India.

Ptolemy married his sister Arsinoe, a common practice in ancient Egypt. Although in modern times it might be considered to be somewhat odd and even against the law, this type of alliance was in good keeping with Egyptian tradition. Pharaohs were living Gods who, therefore, could only marry living Goddesses, often their sisters.

After they were united, the two were known as Ptolemy Philadelphos (Sister-Lover); and Arsinoe Philadelpha, (Brother-Lover). I would like to suggest yet another epithet, which I fell suits them just as well. This is a word that I have just created and is therefore useless to look it up in a dictionary. The word for dog in ancient Greek is: kuwv, kuvos (from which the word Cynic originated). I would like to describe Arsinoe and Ptolemy as Philokynoi—Dog Lovers!

Whether the Dachshund is native or imported to Egypt is an open question. During the twelfth Dynasty other countries were subjugated by Egypt and the Dachshund could have been brought in from an adjoining country. Salukis, Greyhounds, and Besenjis were also plentiful and most who write about Dachshunds admit to those Hound's presence. One should note that those hounds were working and sporting dogs; they are represented participating in the hunt or actively engaged in battles.

Dachshund-types did not escape the Greeks either. Xenophon describes the Agasso as very Dachshund-like, and the cynologist (a student of dog science) Arrian of Bithynia (a part of Turkey) did the same with his Canis castorius.

These observations appear to suggest that since we have no proof, we must assume that Dachshunds began to evolve in the sixteenth century. The very reasons that Meistrell cites for not being able to trace them to the ancient Egyptians, i.e., "Egyptian artists ignored relative proportions altogether," and "The work of these artists was so highly stylized as to be distorted" may ironically be the very reasons why these depictions could indeed be representations of Dachshund ancestors. We must remember that the earliest known breeds of dogs were developed for utilitarian purposes, not as docile creatures to adorn laps.

The Romans also used short, digging dogs as well as ferrets for small game, some proof of which is Hilzheimer's discovery of two Dachshund-like skeletons in a Roman ruin near Stuttgart, Germany.

Further claims regarding the breed's existence in antiquity are based upon stone, wood, and clay models of short-legged animals found in Peru, Mexico, Greece, and China. Judging from photographs and sketches of these sculptures, it would take a wild flight of fancy to seriously identify them as Dachshunds. Some look more like pigs.

The Dachshund in the Dark and Middle Ages

The Dachshund may have passed from Egypt to Europe and to Asia as well. Earlier in this chapter, David Blum recounted the depiction of a Dachshund-like dog dated 1323, discovered on a tomb in England. The image is striking in its similarity to the Standard we know today.

Sending the legions packing, Germanic tribes preserved some of the invader's low-slung dogs, or may have bred them with indigenous dogs. During the 800s, Charlemagne kept various types of dogs, including kennels of beaver or badger dogs.

More definite evidence of Dachshunds comes from the early 1400s, with the tombs of Anna von Bickenbach and Knebel von Katzenbogen in Katherine's Church, Oppenheim, Germany. As dogs often kept their owner's feet warm in bed, so they often ended up at those same feet in tomb art. Evidence appears outside of Europe as well. A Korean brush painting by Yi Am dated 1499, owned by the San Francisco Museums of Art, is clearly of a Dachshund mother and her puppies.

Dachshunds from the Seventeenth Century through the Present

Certainly the breeds, as we have come to recognize them today, owe a great deal to breeding in Germany during the seventeenth and eighteenth centuries. In the nineteenth century, August and Wilhelm von Daake were known for their careful breeding to produce a dog that worked above and below ground. In general, wired and longhaired appeared to be better suited for hunting tasks involving overland work, trailing game, etc. The smooth Dachshund was an earthdog—digging, disappearing into the dens of their prey, and either ferreting the hunted animals or holding them at bay until their masters arrived on the scene.

This kind of breeding would be in direct contrast with the Egyptian representations of the Dachshund as an elegant pet that acted as a companion to the ruling class. In a way, the German breeding and the ample documentation of the hunting development of the Dachshund would work against most Dachshund fanciers' desire to see the Dachshund in any other light. If one is to assume that hunting dogs had a higher status, then it would follow that one might not "see" a Dachshund in the tomb paintings in a position of importance as she, in fact, is represented. Therefore, the first Dachshund did not have to be a hunter. Her proximity to the throne and her master is actually a greater compliment, and suggests that a very special, spiritual bond must have existed and been so important as to earn her, not only visual representation, but also immortality on tomb walls.

Iris Love has said that although she has devoted her life to past history, her concern is for the future history of the Dachshund. Her thoughts are echoed by every person who has contributed to this book, as well as by every responsible breeder and owner. Irresponsible breeding for color or profit cannot and must not be tolerated. If we have convinced you to own a Dachshund we implore that you purchase her from a reputable breeder. If you already own one, and are considering breeding him or her, please consult with a member of the Dachshund Club of America before proceeding. We, as responsible Dachshund owners, are making every effort to eradicate past diseases, and to help prevent new ones. We need your help. We are our Dachshund's keepers.

Glossary

THE AMERICAN KENNEL CLUB (AKC): Founded in 1884, a nonprofit corporation devoted to the advancement of purebred dogs. It maintains a registry of recognized breeds; adopts and enforces rules and regulations governing dog shows, Obedience Trials, and Field Trials; fosters and encourages interest in, and the health and welfare of, purebred dogs.

ANGULATION: In the forequarters, the angles formed by the shoulder, arm, forearm, wrist, pastern, and toes. In the hindquarters, the angles formed by the hip, thigh, second thigh, hock, pastern, and toes. As defined in the Dachshund Standard, correct angulation is most desirable. Straight fronts with little or no angulation from the shoulder through the arm to the toes, while common, is undesirable.

BALANCE: The overall picture of the dog as viewed from the side or while in motion. No features should be prominent or exaggerated. Each part should flow naturally into the next and work in harmony with one another.

BARREL HOCKS: The rear hocks turned out, causing the feet and toes to turn inward.

BEADY: Describes round and small eyes often found in Miniatures. The Dachshund eye should be almond-shaped both in the Standard and Miniature.

BEARD: Hairgrowth on the underjaw characteristic of the wirehair.

BITCH: A female Daschund.

BITE: The position of the upper and lower teeth relative to one another when the jaws are together. The preferable bite for the Dachshund is scissors, but level is acceptable. It should never be undershot or overshot.

BLACK AND TAN: A common, recognized color in Dachshunds. It is characterized by a predominantly black coat with tan markings generally around the eyes, chin, feet, and under the tail.

BLUE AND TAN: A recognized Dachshund color. Solid steel-gray with tan points or markings.

BLUE SLIP: AKC Dog Registration Application.

BONE: Describes the proportion and structure of the shoulders, legs, and ribs relative to the size of the dog.

BRINDLE: A marking or pattern characterized by striping.

BROCK: A badger, the Dachshund's preferred prey.

BROOD BITCH: A female used for repeated breedings producing quality puppies generally with easy deliveries.

BRUSH: A bushy or hairy tail.

CHAMPION: A title awarded by the AKC to dogs achieving predetermined points in conformation or various trial shows licensed by the AKC. A Ch. preceding a dog's name in a certified pedigree is most desirable when purchasing a puppy.

CHOCOLATE (CHOCOLATE AND TAN): A recognized color in Dachshunds, it is characterized by a chocolate-brown color with tan points. When compared with reds, chocolates have tan rims around the eyes, and reds have black rims.

COARSE: A relative term used to describe the overall appearance of the dog. A coarse dog tends to be exaggerated in appearance where the distinguishable parts create the whole. In refined Dachshund, which is preferred, the parts flow together subtly and uniformly.

CONFORMATION: The basic skeletal and muscular structure of the dog and its relationship to the Standard.

COW-HOCKED: The rear hocks (elbows) turn inward, causing the hind feet and toes to turn outward.

CREAM: A recognized color in Dachshunds, distinguishable as a very light cream, gold, or blond color. Not to be confused with light red, which is classified as red.

CRYPTORCHID: A mature male with one or both testicles undescended into the scrotum but retained in the abdomen. Cryptorchidism is a disqualifying fault.

DAM: A mother Dachshund and the female parent.

DAPPLE: A marking distinguishable by randomly spaced patches of lighter colors or hues of the base color. No pattern exists, and the patches may be in a ragged pattern.

DEWCLAW: A fifth toe, which is considered extraneous and functionless, but not considered undesirable.

DOG: A male Dachshund.

DOUBLE DAPPLE: A marking similar in appearance to the dapple but with varying amounts of pure white on the body.

DRIVE: Strong thrusting of the hindquarters while moving forward, denoting soundness and correct muscle and bone structure. A positive attribute in Dachshunds.

EAST-WEST FRONT: A structural fault causing the toes and feet to turn outward. While undesirable, an ever so slight turning outward is acceptable.

EXPRESSION: The overall appearance of the head. A blending of the correct parts in the Standard indicates a good expression. Often a contributing factor in determining refinement or coarseness.

FAWN: A recognized Dachshund color distinguishable as brown and reddish-yellow in appearance, similar to the underbelly of a deer.

FIDDLE FRONT: Describes a condition in which the elbows on the forequarters protrude outward, the pasterns are close together, and the feet turn outward. Picture a Chippendale table leg. Definitely not desirable.

FOREARM: The area between the elbow and the wrist. It should be straight but wrap comfortably around the chest.

FOREQUARTERS: The front arm or leg assembly from the shoulder blade to the feet.

FRONT: One of the four major sections (namely, the head, front, body, and rear) of the dog. It includes the neck, chest, forequarters, and brisket.

GAIT: Rhythm of the dog in motion. The movement of the fore- and hindquarters and the placement of the feet at varying rates of speed.

GAY TAIL: A tail carried above the topline often curling forward. This should be considered a fault in Dachshunds.

GESTATION: The time from conception to birth. Normally sixty-three days duration, but anywhere between fifty-nine and sixty-five is not uncommon.

HINDQUARTERS: The back leg assembly from the shoulders to the feet.

HOCK: The joint between the second thigh and the pastern. Equivalent to the heel in humans.

HOCKS WELL LET DOWN: The hock joint near to the ground. Excellent attribute in the Dachshund.

HONORABLE SCARS: Scars received from injuries while working. These are to be considered acceptable.

INBREEDING: The practice of breeding closely related males and females. In effect, incest. While acceptable, it is not widely practiced and should be done only by knowledgeable breeders under unique circumstances.

ISABELLA: Another term for the Fawn color (isabella and tan).

KEEL: The lower chest from the breastbone to the ribs.

KNUCKLING OVER: A faulty movement of the wrist joint, permitting its forward movement under the weight of the dog. A disqualifying fault in Dachshunds.

LAYBACK: The angle of the shoulder and upper arm as compared to the vertical. A Dachshund lacking in layback will have a straight front, which is undesirable. Layback is essential for digging and movement when going to ground.

LEAD: A leash used in the show ring. Several types are available.

LEVEL BITE: Both upper and lower front teeth meet exactly, with neither overriding the other. Scissor is the correct bite in Dachshunds, but level is acceptable.

LIMITED REGISTRATION: An option available to the breeder when transferring ownership when signing the Blue Slip. It permits registration of the dog with the AKC, but excludes registration of its offspring. Used when the breeder does not want to perpetuate existing faults or is concerned that the dog may be used to breed for profit.

LINE BREEDING: Breeding within the same line or family ancestry as in mating with a granddam or grandsire or others within a pedigree. *See* OUT-CROSSING.

LOIN: Section of the body between the ribs and the hindquarters.

LONGHAIR: One of three varieties of Dachshunds characterized by a long coat as opposed to a smooth or wire coat.

METATARSUS: Rear pastern.

MINIATURE: In Dachshunds, any dog weighing under eleven pounds at one year of age.

MONORCHID: A mature male with one testicle undescended into the scrotum. A disqualifying fault.

MUZZLE: That part of the head in front of and below the eyes. Essentially the nose and jaws.

OUT AT ELBOWS: Loose shoulders jutting outward. Undesirable in Dachshunds.

OUTCROSSING: Within the same breed, breeding with unrelated dogs not within the same pedigree. *See* LINE BREEDING.

OVAL CHEST: One deeper than it is wide. Desirable in Dachshunds.

OVERSHOT: Describes a jaw in which incisors or six upper front teeth extend over the lower incisors, creating a space between the upper and lower teeth when the jaw is closed. A fault.

PADDLING: A condition in which the forward legs appear to move in a stiff outward motion, resulting from a lack of upper arm.

PAD: The sole of the foot.

PEDIGREE: A document showing a dog's lineage through several generations, including its dam and sire, grand- and great-granddams and sires. This may be an unofficial document unless certified by the AKC.

PET QUALITY: A term used by breeders to denote that a dog is not of show quality (i.e., it has faults or qualities which are not deemed acceptable in the conformation show ring). Buyers of pet-quality dogs from a reputable breeder need not be concerned about the animal's health or longevity as a pet.

PIED: Fairly large patches of two or more colors. In Dachshunds, piebald. See Chapter 8 on color. It is important to note that the United States is the only country that recognizes this pattern. In all other countries it is a disqualification. The authors do not encourage perpetuation of this breeding due to current and future health problems.

PIGEON-TOED: Toes point inward. Not desirable in Dachshunds.

PINCER BITE: Same as level.

PROFESSIONAL HANDLER: One who accepts a fee to show a dog.

PUREBRED: A dog produced by two parents of the same breed, neither of which have ever been interbred with breeds other than their own species. Generally registered with the AKC in the United States.

PUT DOWN: An expression used among exhibitors and handlers at conformation dog shows denoting the preparation and appearance of a dog in the ring after bathing and grooming. Also a synonym for euthanasia.

QUALITY: Describes a dog exhibiting excellence in conformation and representation of the breed.

REAR: The hindquarters. One of four major sections of a dog, namely head, front, body, and rear.

RED: The most popular of the recognized Dachshund colors. Any shade or hue of brown. Not to be confused with cream, fawn, or sable.

REFINED: Elegant and graceful in appearance. The opposite of coarse. Each individual part of the dog flows smoothly into the next with no discernible connection.

REGISTER: To record a dog's breeding to include sire and dam and other required information as contained on the Blue Slip.

ROACH BACK: A convex curve of the back along the loin between the front and rear. Undesirable in Dachshunds. The topline should be level.

ROMAN NOSE: A convex curve of the nasal area between the nostrils and the eyes. A slight roman nose is preferred in the Dachshund, an exaggerated convex or concave nose is not.

SABLE: A marking or pattern. Very rare, and not to be confused with red. Found only in the longhair variety, there is a lighter red undercoat with a black overlay. A widow's peak or dark mask is found around the eyes. Many puppies exhibit these characteristics but turn completely red as they mature. One should delay registration to determine if the pattern remains.

SCISSORS BITE: The correct Dachshund bite. The outside of the lower incisors meet the inside of the upper incisors. Not to be confused with overshot, where a space exists between the two, and results in a fault.

SHOW QUALITY: In the breeder's opinion, a dog that exhibits characteristics consistent with the Standard, making it capable of attaining Champion.

SIRE: A father Daschund and the male parent.

SMOOTH: One of the three varieties of Dachshunds characterized by a short, smooth coat.

SNIPY: A pointed and narrow muzzle not in balance with the skull. Often common in the Dachshund, it is not desirable.

STANDARD: The larger of the two Dachshund sizes. Also, the conformation description of the Dachshund approved by the Dachshund Club of America.

STOP: The area around the eyes where the muzzle and the skull meet.

STUD DOG: A male of show quality used for breeding.

TEMPERAMENT: A dog's inherent nature. Established at birth, it may be affected by environment.

Topline: The top or back of the dog from the shoulders to the rear with a natural extension to the neck and the tail. Viewed from the side, a Dachshund should have a level topline with no convex or concave curve.

Type: One's interpretation of the ideal Dachshund from the Standard. Also, characteristics that remain consistent from one dog to the next in the eye of the breeder or judge.

Undershot: Describes a jaw in which the incisors or six lower front teeth extend forward of the upper incisors, creating a space between the upper and lower teeth when the jaw is closed. Opposite of overshot, this is a fault in Dachshunds.

Variety: Any one of three types of Dachshund, namely smooth, longhair, and wirehair.

Walleye: An eye characterized by a white, blue, or pearl-coloring. Dachshunds should have a dark eye. They may occur in dapples.

Wheaton: A recognized Dachshund color found in wirehairs. A very light red with darker color on the ends of the coat. Similar to the color of a Soft-Coated Wheaten Terrier.

Wild Boar: A Dachshund color, characteristic of the wirehair. A black or dark outer coat laid over a lighter undercoat.

Wirehair: One of the three varieties of Dachshunds characterized by a wiry textured coat.

Withers: The highest point of the shoulder blades.

Directory

Unfortunately, there is no easy way to provide a comprehensive directory of names, addresses, and telephone numbers. The only fully-staffed dog organization is the American Kennel Club, and although we provide its current address, it is moving to North Carolina, so that address will change.

Individual breed clubs are run by volunteers from their homes, and since most are elected by their respective clubs, contacts change.

Our best advice is to contact the AKC and they will give you a name and number to call.

If you are interested in membership in the Dachshund Club of America, contact the secretary and request an application. Once completed, you will have to meet and be sponsored by two members. DCA publishes a newsletter four times a year of general interest to all.

NATIONAL ORGANIZATIONS

American Kennel Club
51 Madison Avenue
New York, NY 10010

Dachshund Club of America
c/o David Faust
601 Englehart Drive
Madison, WI 53713

REGIONAL ORGANIZATIONS

Alabama Dachshund Club, Inc.
Albany Capital District Dachshund Club (NY)
Badger Dachshund Club (WI)
Bay Colony Dachshund Club, Inc. (MA)
Bayou Dachshund Club of New Orleans, Inc.
Cascade Dachshund Club (WA)
Central Ohio Dachshund Club, Inc.
Columbine Dachshund Club (CO)
Connecticut Yankee Dachshund Club
Dachshund Association of Long Island
Dachshund Club of California
Dachshund Club of the Great Lakes
Dachshund Club of Greater Buffalo
Dachshund Club of Greater Syracuse
Dachshund Club of Hawaii
Dachshund Club of Metropolitan Atlanta
Dachshund Club of New Jersey
Dachshund Club of St. Louis
Dachshund Club of Santa Ana Valley, Inc.
Dachshund Club of Southwestern Ohio, Inc.
Dachshund Fanciers Association of Berks County (PA)
Dallas-Ft. Worth Dachshund Club
Desert Valley Dachshund Club (AZ)
East Bay Dachshund Club (CA)
Florida East Coast Dachshund Club
Florida Gulf Coast Dachshund Club
Golden Gate Dachshund Club
Greater Portland Dachshund Club
Heart of America Dachshund Club (KS)
Hoosier Dachshund Club, Inc. (IN)
Houston Dachshund Club
Hudson Valley Dachshund Association (NY)
Knickerbocker Dachshund Club (NY)
Lincolnland Dachshund Club (IL)
Louisville Dachshund Club, Inc.
Metropolitan Baltimore Dachshund Club
Metropolitan Washington Dachshund Club (DC)
Midwest Dachshund Club (MI)
Minnesota Dachshund Club, Inc.
Mission City Dachshund Club (TX)
New Mexico Dachshund Club
Northern California Dachshund Club

San Diego Dachshund Club, Inc.
Sierra Dachshund Breeders Club (CA)
Sooner Dachshund Club (OK)
Sunshine Dachshund Club of Jackonsville, Inc. (FL)
Western Pennsylvania Dachshund Club
Dachshund Fanciers of Central Virginia